PRESENTED TO:

....

FROM:

....

DATE:

....

100 DEVOTIONS

faith forward

Family Devotional

ZONDERVAN
Faith Forward Family Devotional

Copyright © 2019 by Patrick Schwenk and Ruth Schwenk

This title is also available as a Zondervan ebook.

Requests for information should be addressed to:

Zondervan, 3900 Sparks Dr. SE, Grand Rapids, Michigan 49546

ISBN 978-0-310-45314-7

Authors are represented by the literary agency of The Fedd Agency, Inc., P. O. Box 341973, Austin, Texas, 78734.

Art direction: Patti Evans
Interior design: Kristy Edwards

Printed in China

19 20 21 22 23 DSC 10 9 8 7 6 5 4 3 2 1

100 DEVOTIONS

faith forward

Family Devotional

❋

Ruth & Patrick
Schwenk

ZONDERVAN®
.com

CONTENTS

• • • • • • • • •

LETTER TO PARENTS

• • • • • • • • •

Dear parents,

One of the greatest joys we have in life is the calling, with God's help, to shape our children's hearts. To ground them, guard them, and guide them in God's amazing truth, love, and grace. And of course, to one day release our children into the world for God's glory!

Written for families with children of all ages, *Faith Forward Family Devotional* takes families like yours through the entire Bible in one hundred devotions. Each devotion is complete with key verses, a devotion for the whole family, a key idea, discussion questions geared for various ages, and even a family prayer.

Faith Forward Family Devotional is the perfect resource for everyday busy parents who also desire to help pass on faith to the next generation. Simple, practical, conversational, and full of God's truth, it is written to help families, with kids of all ages, keep God at the center of who they are and what they do!

Our prayer is that you not only come to know God's Word more fully, but that you also come to trust Jesus more faithfully. That you would know the power and presence of God's Spirit. And that you and your family would be light in the dark!

We, too, want to see faith move forward in our family and in the world. We know it's not always easy. It's not always convenient. But our calling is critical. And so we hope that this devotional is a blessing to you and your family. We trust it will further equip you and inspire you to help raise another generation to love and serve Jesus.

Passing on faith with you!

Patrick and Ruth Schwenk

GOD CREATES

• • • • • • • • •

In the beginning God created the heavens and the earth. Now the earth was formless and empty, darkness was over the surface of the deep, and the Spirit of God was hovering over the waters.

GENESIS 1:1–2

How did you start your day today? Maybe you jumped out of bed, eager to play outside. Did your mom or dad drag you out of bed to get ready for school? Or maybe your day began with something to eat or a list of chores.

When we first open the Bible, we discover a different kind of beginning—the *very* beginning. The start of it all. Not just the start of a day, not just the beginning of a new week, but the beginning of God's creation. The beginning of God's work in the world. The beginning of everything!

In five simple but important words, we read, "In the beginning God created." Nothing came before God! He was the beginning, and everything else comes from Him. He is the Author and Giver of life. God created "the heavens and the earth."

God our Father created the light and separated it from the darkness. He called the light "day" and darkness "night." He separated the water above from the water below, calling it "sky." God gathered the water under the sky and caused dry ground to appear. And then He began to fill what He created.

KEY IDEA

God is powerful. It takes a lot of faith to believe that He created something from nothing. The Bible teaches that God is the Creator of all things. Out of nothing, He made everything!

The dry ground was filled with plants and all kinds of vegetation.

The sky was filled with the sun, moon, and countless stars.

Living creatures filled the seas, dry ground, and blue sky.

Then God made man and woman—in His own image.

He made everything from nothing.

From the very beginning, God was creating a world where He could be known. A world to be enjoyed by His creation. And that was just the beginning! Soon we'll see how God is creating a world where we are invited to join Him in all He is doing.

LET'S DISCUSS TOGETHER

- *Describe a time when you have seen God's power or strength in your own life.*
- *Why is it important to believe that God created us?*
- *In what areas of your life do you need to remember that God is powerful and He is with you?*

LET'S PRAY TOGETHER

Father, You are our Creator. You are almighty—powerful and strong. We were made by You and for You. Help us trust that You are powerful, strong, and in control of all that happens. We love You and want to live for Your purposes. In Jesus' name, amen.

● ● ● ● ● ● ●

For Further Study: Genesis 1:1–31

2

FRIENDSHIP WITH GOD

• • • • • • • • •

God said, "Let us make mankind in our image, in our likeness, so
that they may rule over the fish in the sea and the birds in the
sky, over the livestock and all the wild animals, and over all the
creatures that move along the ground."

GENESIS 1:26

Have you ever made something you were really proud of? What was
it, and why did you make it? God is a creative God. Full of power.
Overflowing with goodness and wisdom. And that's not all! God's love
is the source of all He has made.

The Bible teaches that love has always existed between God the
Father, the Son, and the Holy Spirit. Love just pours out of God because
love is who He is! Do you know what the best part is? God created us to
share in His love by being in a relationship with Him.

When God was finished creating the heavens and earth, filling it
with every kind of living creature, He saved the best for last. He made
human beings in His image. Not even angels or animals are said to be
made in God's image. There is something special about who we are and
the kind of relationship we can have with God.

We are made to be in a loving friendship with God in which we listen
to Him, trust Him, and obey what He says. God gives us emotions to feel,

KEY IDEA

God is relational. The Bible teaches that God is Father, Son, and Holy Spirit. He has always existed in relationship. He created us to live in a relationship with Himself by faith in Jesus, through the power of the Holy Spirit.

a mind to think, and a will to freely love God the way He first loved us.

Only a friendship with God can truly make us happy. It's a friendship that promises joy, peace, and hope that will never go away!

LET'S DISCUSS TOGETHER

- *In what ways do we share God's "likeness"?*
- *Why is being in a relationship with God necessary for showing others what God is like?*
- *What are one or two practical ways you can begin showing others what God is like?*

LET'S PRAY TOGETHER

Father, You have made us to be in a relationship with You through faith in Your Son, Jesus. Continue to teach us. Grow us. Make us more like You by making us more like Jesus. Fill us with Your Holy Spirit so we can show others what You are really like. In Jesus' name, amen.

• • • • • • •

For Further Study: Genesis 1:26–28; Colossians 1:15; Colossians 3:9–10

6

3

PARTNERS WITH GOD

• • • • • • • • •

The Lord God took the man and put him in the Garden of Eden to work it and take care of it.

GENESIS 2:15

How do you usually respond when your mom or dad asks you to help around the house? Are you ready to serve or ready to complain? The story of creation is a reminder that God not only loves us but also invites us to work with Him and for Him.

When God first created Adam and Eve, He placed them in the perfect home. It was called the garden of Eden or the garden of delight. It was perfect in every way because God was present there with Adam and Eve.

There was no sin. No fighting. No crying. People didn't get hurt, lonely, or scared. There was no death or sadness. Just pure love and joy and peace. It was like heaven on earth! But God had a job for Adam and Eve to do. God created them to work—to help take care of His creation.

In God's eyes, work is good. It is important and full of meaning. Work isn't something bad or something to complain about. In fact, God has given each of us different gifts or abilities. God created us to join Him in His work of telling the world what He is like.

Our work might be something around the house, like putting away the dishes, mowing the grass, or doing laundry. Or someday it could be a job as a teacher, doctor, or engineer. Whatever we do, we can do it with an even greater purpose. We can do it to love others and show people what God is like. God doesn't want our work to be a chore. He wants it to be a chance for us to serve people and bring glory to Him.

LET'S DISCUSS TOGETHER

- *How do you usually respond to work?*
- *How can work be a way of showing other people what God is like?*
- *How can you use your gifts and abilities to love other people?*

LET'S PRAY TOGETHER

Father, give us the same attitude of Jesus—an attitude of love toward others. Help us remember that no matter what we do, we are really serving You. Teach us to work hard and to work to bless and serve those around us. In Jesus' name, amen.

• • • • • • •

For Further Study: Genesis 2:4–17

4

SEPARATION

· · · · · · · · ·

The Lord God made garments of skin for Adam and his wife and clothed them.

GENESIS 3:21

Everything in God's creation was just right. Perfect. But then something terrible happened.

It turns out God has an Enemy. This Enemy, Satan, used to be a friend. He was once a powerful and beautiful angel. But Satan didn't want to love God; Satan wanted to *be* God.

Satan knew God was powerful and that God wanted to use His creation to tell the whole world what He was like. He wanted to stop God's plan from the very beginning.

He came disguised as a snake, telling lies about God. He tried to trick Adam and Eve into believing that God wasn't good. That God didn't really love them. And that life would be better if they were in charge, doing what they wanted, instead of trusting and obeying their Father and Friend.

It worked too. Even though God had given Adam and Eve everything they could have wanted, it wasn't enough. They disobeyed the one command God gave them: "You must not eat from the tree of the knowledge of good and evil" (Genesis 2:17). If they ate from it, God warned, they would not enjoy a long and amazing life with God forever. Instead of friendship with God, they would experience separation. That's exactly what happened.

After eating the fruit, Adam and Eve felt guilty for the first time. They realized they were naked, so they hid from God. But because of God's great love, God clothed them with animal skins. It was like He was wrapping their sin with His love. Even though they would have to leave their perfect home, they would not lose their perfect Father and Friend. He would never stop loving them.

God was just beginning His work in the world. The story of Adam and Eve is a reminder that we too have an Enemy. He might not come disguised as a snake, but Satan is still trying to break up people's friendship with God and to stop His work in the world. But we know God has something so much better for us when we trust and obey Him!

LET'S DISCUSS TOGETHER

- *Describe a time when you were tempted not to obey God.*
- *As we live for God, how can we guard against Satan's temptations?*

- *The good news is that we are not alone. How do you think God protects us?*

LET'S PRAY TOGETHER

Father, thank You that You never leave us or stop loving us, even when we sin. Help us be wise and not fearful in fighting against Satan's temptations. Protect us. Give us the strength to trust You and obey You. In Jesus' name, amen.

● ● ● ● ● ●

For Further Study: Genesis 3:1–24

5

FAMILY TROUBLE: CAIN AND ABEL

• • • • • • • • •

The Lord said to Cain, "Why are you angry? Why is your face downcast? If you do what is right, will you not be accepted? But if you do not do what is right, sin is crouching at your door; it desires to have you, but you must rule over it."

GENESIS 4:6-7

You don't have to live very long to learn that sometimes it's hard to get along with other people—even the people we love, like family or friends. Does this sound familiar to you? What do you and your siblings fight about?

The good news is that there are no perfect families. In fact, the only perfect family that ever existed—Adam and Eve—didn't stay perfect for long!

As they began to build a family outside of the garden, Genesis 4 tells us that Adam and Eve would have two sons: Cain and Abel. Cain would grow up to be a farmer, working with the soil. Abel would become a shepherd, taking care of flocks of sheep.

One day each of them brought an offering (or gift) to God. Cain gave some of his crops, but Abel gave the best of his flocks. God was not pleased with Cain's gift, but He was very happy with Abel's. How do you think Cain responded? Not very well!

Cain grew angry . . . so angry that he eventually killed his brother, Abel. The Lord asked him, "Where is your brother?" But Cain lied and said, "I don't know. Am I my brother's keeper?" Sin was pulling Cain further and further away from God. And sin was hurting what God wanted to do through them.

Cain never did say he was sorry. He only complained when God told him he would have to leave and wander from place to place, far from his home. Cain would eventually get married and start a family of his own. God would bless Adam and Eve with another son named Seth, who would have a family of his own too. God was far from done showing the world what He is like.

But we have to be careful of how sin can pull us apart. Not only does sin hurt our relationship with our Father, but it also hurts our relationships with one another. So be on guard. Watch out. Don't let sin get in the way of loving God and loving others!

LET'S DISCUSS TOGETHER

- *Why do you think God was not pleased with Cain's offering?*
- *What made Abel's offering acceptable?*
- *In what ways can our separation from God lead to separation from one another?*

LET'S PRAY TOGETHER

Father, You are full of love and grace. Even though we sin, You forgive us. We know You want to work through our family. Help us love and serve one another. Protect us. Make our relationships stronger, our love deeper, and our faith stronger. In Jesus' name, amen.

● ● ● ● ● ● ●

For Further Study: Genesis 4:1–26

6

WHEN DIFFERENT IS GOOD: NOAH

• • • • • • • • •

Noah was a righteous man, blameless among the people of his time, and he walked faithfully with God.

GENESIS 6:9

B eing different isn't always bad. In fact, sometimes being different is really good! This is especially true in the story of Noah—a man who was very different from everyone else around him.

As families continued to grow and people continued to spread out on the earth, people's sin grew too. Genesis 6 tells us that people grew further away from God. Fewer and fewer people wanted to be friends with God. Many didn't want to know God, let alone live for Him. God's heart was sad because of people's sin.

But there was one man who was different. Noah stood out. As God was preparing to deal with people's sin, He found one man who was living righteously. Even though everyone else was doing what was wrong, Noah was living right. He was a man of faith. And because of Noah's faith, he "found favor in the eyes of the LORD" (Genesis 6:8).

The Lord told Noah to build an ark, a huge boat that would be a temporary home to Noah and his family. And as it turns out, it was home not only for his family but for a lot of animals too! Two of every kind, male and female. Noah did everything the Lord told him to do.

KEY IDEA

God is holy and just but gracious. God is completely without sin. Because He is holy, He has to deal with sin. Every time God deals with sin, He also shows His grace (His undeserved love). He gives people an opportunity to turn *from* their sin and turn *to* Him for help. The ark is an example of God's showing His love even when people were running from Him.

Drop by drop, the rain began to fall—until finally, the earth was flooded. For forty days and forty nights, it rained and rained and rained! Every living creature left on earth died. But Noah and his family and the animals in the ark were safe, warm, and dry.

God did not forget Noah and his family. He began to push back the water, slowly drying it up, until one day it was finally safe to leave the ark. God made a promise that He would never again destroy the earth with a flood. He put a rainbow in the sky as a reminder of the promise He made to Noah.

God is still looking for people to be different—men and women and boys and girls who are willing to walk by faith. Will you be the one to stand out and listen to God, even when no one else does?

LET'S DISCUSS TOGETHER

- *Why did God choose to send rain to flood the earth?*
- *Why do you think God told Noah to build an ark?*
- *What do those things say about who God is?*

LET'S PRAY TOGETHER

Father, You are holy. You are completely without sin. But You are also full of love, always giving us a chance to turn to You. Help us be different like Noah, loving and obeying You even when it is hard. Help us live for You no matter what. In Jesus' name, amen.

● ● ● ● ● ● ●

For Further Study: Genesis 6–9

7

SAY WHAT?

• • • • • • • • •

Come, let us build ourselves a city, with a tower that reaches to the heavens, so that we may make a name for ourselves; otherwise we will be scattered over the face of the whole earth.

GENESIS 11:4

Have you ever done something to make yourself look better in front of other people? We've probably all been tempted to try to impress others. We were made to use our gifts and abilities in creative ways to bring God glory and to bless others. Unfortunately, as we see in Genesis 11, people decided to create something for their own glory or fame.

God's people knew they were supposed to spread out and fill the earth (Genesis 1:28; Genesis 9:1). That was God's plan from the beginning—to send His people out to walk with Him and join His work of telling the world what He is like.

But people had another idea. "Come, let us build a city and tower to make a name for ourselves." Their hearts were full of pride. Instead of living to show other people how great God is, they wanted everyone to know how great they were!

God never lets us stay in our sin for too long. He always wants and works for what is best for us, which is why God could only watch the building project for so long! Up until that point, the people had one language, easily talking to one another. They were united. The problem was that they were united against God! Since God's plan was to tell the whole world what He is like, He confused their language (Genesis 11:9), naming the city Babel.

God was reminding His people that His work in the world must be done His way. We were created for so much more than making a name for ourselves. God loves us and invites us into the most exciting life there is—telling the world how great He is!

LET'S DISCUSS TOGETHER

- *How would you describe pride?*
- *What are ways we can be prideful?*
- *Why is it so important to remember that God's work in the world must be done His way?*

LET'S PRAY TOGETHER

There is no one like You, Lord. You are awesome, faithful, powerful, and loving. Thank You for giving me the gift of life. Help me use my life to live for You and not just me.
In Jesus' name, amen.

• • • • • • •

For Further Study: Genesis 11:1–9

8
WHEN GOD SAYS, "GO!"

• • • • • • • • •

The LORD had said to Abram, "Go from your country, your people and your father's household to the land I will show you."

GENESIS 12:1

Have you ever been asked to do something and you didn't know why? Or have you ever been asked to do something that seemed too hard? Maybe you didn't know how you were going to do it. If so, you are not alone!

From the time Adam and Eve left the garden, things continued to get worse. Cain killed his brother Abel. People were so bad that God sent a flood. And then instead of living for God's glory, people built a city and tower for their own glory. But then we meet a man named Abram and his wife, Sarai. God was about to do something new.

In Genesis 12:1, we read that the Lord said to Abram, "Go from your country, your people and your father's household to the land I will show you." I imagine Abram was thinking to himself, *I don't understand. I am afraid. How can I trust this God?* God was telling him to "Go!" He was to leave his home and go to new land, a promised land, that God would show him only after he took his first steps of faith.

We're told that Abram and Sarai, along with his nephew Lot, went where God told them to go. He was seventy-five years old when he and his family left their home for a new home. In faith, Abram obeyed God even when he didn't completely understand.

When they arrived, the Lord appeared again to Abram and promised him He would give the land of Canaan to his family (Genesis 12:7). They built an altar and worshipped the Lord. Something new was about to happen. God was on the move.

But it all started with faith. God didn't choose Abram because he was perfect. When God told Abram and Sarai to go, they listened and obeyed. God is still looking for that kind of faith today—a faith willing to listen to and obey God even when we don't always understand!

LET'S DISCUSS TOGETHER

- *When have you been asked to do something you didn't understand?*
- *How would you describe faith?*
- *How are Abram and Sarai good examples of what it looks like to live by faith today?*

LET'S PRAY TOGETHER

Lord, thank You for saving us by faith. Help us show our love for You by listening to and obeying You. Even when it is hard or we don't understand why, give us strength to follow You. In Jesus' name, amen.

• • • • • • •

For Further Study: Genesis 12:1–9

GOD MAKES A PROMISE

• • • • • • • • •

Abram believed the LORD, and he credited it to him as righteousness.

GENESIS 15:6

H as someone ever made you a promise? What was the promise? Did the person follow through, or did he or she totally forget?

We've already seen how God told Abram and his wife, Sarai, to go to a land He would show them. But God doesn't forget His promises. And He was not done making promises.

God had told Abram He was going to bless him by making his name great. His family would eventually become a great nation! And if that wasn't enough, the whole world would be blessed someday through Abram and his family. That blessing would come when Jesus came as the Savior of the whole world (Genesis 18:18). God was setting apart a special people, a family, for His special purposes.

All of this sounds great. But there was one small—actually, *big*—problem! Abram and Sarai didn't have any children. Zero. None. How was God going to do what seemed impossible and make their family into a whole nation? We're told in Genesis 15:6 that Abram believed God. Once again, Abram showed his faith, trusting that God is not only a promise maker but a promise keeper.

The Lord always keeps His word. This was true for Abram and Sarai, as we'll see. But it is also true for us today. We can count on all the amazing promises that God has made to *us* throughout the Bible! What seems impossible is always possible with God.

LET'S DISCUSS TOGETHER

- *Describe a time when someone made you a promise.*
- *What kind of questions do you think Abram and Sarai had?*
- *How can God's faithfulness to Abram and Sarai encourage us today?*

LET'S PRAY TOGETHER

Father God, thank You for the many ways You bless us. Thank You for the reminder that You are the same God today. We can trust Your Word no matter what is going on in our lives. We can trust what Your Word says, no matter how we feel. You are faithful, and with You all things are possible. In Jesus' name, amen.

• • • • • • •

For Further Study: Genesis 15:1–21

WHEN WAITING IS HARD

• • • • • • • • •

You are the God who sees me.

GENESIS 16:13

Have you ever had to wait for something you really wanted? What was it, and how long did you have to wait? Waiting is never easy. It takes patience. Trust. Belief that when the time is right, we will receive what we have been waiting for.

As we've seen already, God had made some pretty amazing promises to Abram and Sarai. He was going to bless them with a large family that would eventually become a great nation. They would have their own land. And through the coming of Jesus, the whole world would be blessed.

In Genesis 16, we're told that Abram and Sarai had no children. God had promised them a child. The problem was that He didn't say *when* the child would arrive! So they waited. And they waited some more, until waiting on the Lord was just too much.

Sarai took things into her own hands and decided she would try to help God with His plan. Since she couldn't have children, she gave Abram one of her Egyptian maidservants, named Hagar. Hagar would eventually have a child named Ishmael.

But was this really what God wanted? Absolutely not! We can create a lot of our own problems by not waiting on God's timing.

KEY IDEA

God's timing is perfect. God always does what He says. He is faithful. But He always does it in His timing and in His way. Sometimes it might seem as though God is not going to answer a prayer or fulfill a promise. So we need to wait patiently for God, always relying on His timing. Patience is proof that we trust what God has said.

Even though God would take care of Hagar and Ishmael, this was not the child God had promised to Abram and Sarai. They would have to wait some more! This time they would have to learn to wait the right way. Waiting is never easy. But waiting always shows our faith in God and in God's timing.

LET'S DISCUSS TOGETHER

- *Why is waiting so hard?*
- *How does waiting show our faith in God?*
- *How do we sometimes create our own problems by not waiting on God?*

LET'S PRAY TOGETHER

Father, we praise You for always keeping Your word. You are the God who can do all things. Help us to wait on You. Your timing is always perfect. Teach us to be patient, depending on You to come through so You get the glory You deserve. In Jesus' name, amen.

● ● ● ● ● ● ●

For Further Study: Genesis 16:1–16

11

WORTH THE WAIT

· · · · · · · · ·

The LORD was gracious to Sarah as he had said, and the LORD did for Sarah what he had promised.

GENESIS 21:1

E ven though Abram and Sarai didn't do so well waiting, the Lord still showed His love for them. In fact, while they were waiting on the arrival of the child God had promised them, He gave them new names.

"No longer will you be called Abram; your name will be Abraham, for I have made you a father of many nations" (Genesis 17:5). And Sarai? God changed her name too. "Her name will be Sarah," God said. "I will bless her so that she will be the mother of nations; kings of peoples will come from her" (Genesis 17:15–16).

Abraham was a hundred years old, and Sarah was ninety-nine! And sure enough, when it seemed like the waiting would last forever, God did what He promised. With God, all things are possible. He blessed them with a baby boy—the child He had promised. Abraham gave him the name Isaac. Oh, how they must have cried and celebrated and worshipped!

God was not done with His work in the world. He really was setting apart a family, a people, to help let the whole world know what He is like. The waiting was all a part of God's plan so they would never forget it was

God's power at work in them. Isn't this still true today?

It is God's work. His timing. He is faithful to accomplish all of His plans and purposes. We must wait on Him. Trust Him. Obey Him. Do things His way. Whether we are young or old, His power is at work in us and through us!

LET'S DISCUSS TOGETHER

- *What did waiting on God teach Abraham and Sarah about God's power?*
- *How do you think God rewards our patience?*
- *What danger is there in getting ahead of God's plan or lagging behind God's plan?*

LET'S PRAY TOGETHER

Lord, You always give us more than we deserve. You are faithful and good. Thank You that we can help You by telling others about You. Give us power. Fill us with strength. Work through us as we listen to and obey You. In Jesus' name, amen.

● ● ● ● ● ● ●

For Further Study: Genesis 21:1–7

12

A STRANGE TEST

• • • • • • • • •

Abraham called that place The Lᴏʀᴅ Will Provide. And to this day it is said, "On the mountain of the Lᴏʀᴅ it will be provided."

GENESIS 22:14

What is the hardest test you have ever had to take? Did you pass it or fail it? Maybe it was a test for school or a test for a sport. Some are easy. And some . . . well, some tests are just really hard! Abraham and Sarah were about to face this kind of test.

Theirs was a surprise. No teacher gave them a heads-up. There was no time to prepare. A study guide was not handed out. One day the Lord put a test before them. It was an opportunity either to obey God or to disobey God.

This was going to be one tough test! Especially because it involved the very child they had waited so long to receive. Remember Isaac? He was the child the Lord had promised to give Abraham and Sarah. The promises and blessings God gave to Abraham would be passed on to Isaac.

But now God was asking Abraham to give Isaac back to Him by sacrificing him! One day when Isaac was older, he and his dad hiked to Mount Moriah to build an altar and offer a sacrifice to please God. *Where is the sacrifice?* Isaac wondered. He saw the wood. Materials for

KEY IDEA

God is a Provider. He is the One who supplies all of our needs. One day God would give His Son, Jesus, to take away our sins as the perfect sacrifice.

a fire. But no sacrifice. "The Lord will provide," Abraham assured him. Isaac didn't understand that he was the sacrifice.

But sure enough, just in time, there in a patch of trees was a ram. God had provided the sacrifice. What He wanted was Abraham's heart, his faith. Now the Lord knew that Abraham loved Him more than anything, even more than his own son. He had passed the test!

God blessed him. He rewarded him because of his faith. What God wants from us is our hearts. He wants us to love Him and trust Him more than anything else! For Abraham, that meant being willing to give up Isaac. What is it for you?

LET'S DISCUSS TOGETHER

- *How do tests help us grow?*
- *How do you think Abraham and Sarah's love for God changed after this?*
- *What are things today that can become more important to us than loving God?*

LET'S PRAY TOGETHER

Father, You are our great Provider. You have given us what we need most—the gift of salvation through Jesus. He is our perfect sacrifice. Thank You for loving us so much that You sent Your Son to forgive us. Help us love You more and more each day. In Jesus' name, amen.

• • • • • •

For Further Study: Genesis 22:1–19

WE CANNOT OUTSMART GOD

• • • • • • • • •

The LORD said to [Rebekah], "Two nations are in your womb, and two peoples from within you will be separated; one people will be stronger than the other, and the older will serve the younger."

GENESIS 25:23

Has someone ever tricked you? How did they fool you? While we have probably all experienced being fooled or tricked, the good news is that we serve a God who never gets outsmarted! His plans and purposes never fail.

When Isaac grew up, he married Rebekah. She became pregnant with not one child but two! While her twin boys were still in her womb, God told her that the older son (Esau) would serve the younger (Jacob). In other words, all of the promises and blessings God had given to Abraham and then to Isaac were going to pass on to Jacob, not Esau. This must have seemed backward since it was always the eldest son who received the blessing! But not this time.

When Rebekah gave birth, Esau arrived looking red, with hair all over his body. Jacob came out holding on to Esau's heel! When they were older, Esau was a skillful hunter. Jacob? Not so much! He preferred to hang out at home.

And then the trickery started. Jacob tricked Esau into selling him his birthright for a bowl of hot stew. When Rebekah heard that her husband, Isaac, was going to bless Esau instead of Jacob, she came up with a plan to fool him.

KEY IDEA

God is in control. When we remember that God is in control, we can experience peace and assurance no matter what is going on in our lives. We don't need to try to control things or take matters into our own hands. What God wants from us is to trust Him and obey Him.

She cooked Isaac's favorite meal for Jacob to give to him. Because Isaac was old and his vision was bad, she dressed Isaac in Esau's clothing. Rebekah even covered the smooth parts of Isaac's neck and arms with hairy goatskin! The trick worked. Isaac blessed Jacob instead of blessing Esau.

But here's the thing. It was God's plan all along to bless Jacob, not Esau. All of their trickery showed a lack of faith and trust that God was in control. They didn't need to try to fool anyone. They needed to follow what God had already said!

God's plans and purposes always succeed. Our job is to trust and obey what God has said. Where do you need to remember that God is in control?

LET'S DISCUSS TOGETHER

- *In what ways did Rebekah show a lack of faith?*
- *How about Isaac?*
- *Why is it so important to remember that God's purposes never fail?*

LET'S PRAY TOGETHER

Lord, You are in control. All we need to do is trust You. Help us not to worry or try to take things into our own hands. Teach us to wait on You, surrender to Your plans, and obey what You have already told us in Your Word. Your plans and purposes always prevail. In Jesus' name, amen.

● ● ● ● ●

For Further Study:
Genesis 25; Genesis 27

14

EVERYONE HAS A CHOICE

• • • • • • • • •

Jacob made a vow, saying, "If God will be with me and will watch over me on this journey I am taking and will give me food to eat and clothes to wear so that I return safely to my father's household, then the LORD will be my God."

GENESIS 28:20-21

E sau wasn't very happy that Jacob had tricked him out of his birthright, deceived their father, Isaac, and stolen his blessing. So Jacob, fearing for his life, ran away, far away from his family.

One night Jacob rested his head on a stone and fell asleep under the stars. Deep in sleep, he had a rather unusual dream. He saw a big stairway reaching all the way up to heaven. He saw angels. They were climbing up and down the stairway.

But most importantly, the Lord spoke to Jacob in his dream—making Jacob a promise he couldn't ignore. The Lord said to him, "I am the God of Abraham and Isaac. I will give you and your descendants this land. Your descendants will be like the dust of the earth. And all people on earth will be blessed through you. I will be with you and will watch over you."

When Jacob woke up, he was in awe of God. He took the stone he had been sleeping on and built an altar to worship the Lord. He had a choice to make. It's a choice we all have to make. Will the Lord be *my* God? Will I join God's work in the world and walk by faith like Abraham and Isaac did? The answer for Jacob was yes! He didn't always do things perfectly. But Jacob made a decision that the Lord would be *his* God too.

LET'S DISCUSS TOGETHER

- *What did God promise Jacob in his dream?*
- *What does Jacob's response to his dream tell us about his faith?*
- *What was the choice Jacob had to make?*

LET'S PRAY TOGETHER

Lord, we want to follow You. Each day, help us love You and honor You in all we do. Thank You that You are always with us, watching over us and caring for us. In Jesus' name, amen.

● ● ● ● ● ●

For Further Study: Genesis 28

15

THE DECEIVER GETS DECEIVED

• • • • • • • • •

Jacob said to Laban, "What is this you have done to me? I served you for Rachel, didn't I? Why have you deceived me?"

GENESIS 29:25

Have you ever been corrected for something you did wrong? It might not always feel like it, but correction isn't meant to hurt us; it's meant to help us. And this is exactly what would happen to Jacob when he traveled to his uncle Laban's house.

Laban had two daughters. The older was Leah. The younger was Rachel. Jacob was in love with Rachel. She was beautiful in every way. So beautiful that Jacob agreed to work seven—yes, seven—long years to marry her. He loved her so much that those seven years felt like only a few days.

The problem was that Laban tricked him. Now Jacob was the one who was deceived! Instead of giving Rachel to Jacob, Laban gave his other daughter, Leah, to Jacob, disguised in a veil. Jacob wasn't done though. If you thought seven years was a long time, well, Jacob worked another seven years to finally marry Rachel too. So after fourteen years, Jacob had two wives and eventually thirteen children—twelve sons and one daughter.

The Lord was continuing to fulfill His promise to bless Abraham, then Isaac, and now Jacob by increasing his family. His family was growing bigger and bigger. But God was doing something else as well. He was working on Jacob's character. He was working to change the kind of person Jacob was.

God wants to use all our circumstances to help change us. God loves us too much to leave us the way we are. God wasn't finished working on Jacob, and He's not finished working on us either!

LET'S DISCUSS TOGETHER

- *Describe a time when you were corrected. How was it a good thing?*
- *How was God using Laban to try to change Jacob?*
- *What lesson do you think God wanted Jacob to learn?*

LET'S PRAY TOGETHER

Father, change all of us. Take our thoughts, attitudes, words, and actions and help them be pleasing to You. Make us more into the people You want us to be. In Jesus' name, amen.

● ● ● ● ● ● ●

For Further Study: Genesis 29-30

16

JACOB GETS A NEW NAME

• • • • • • • • •

The man said, "Your name will no longer be Jacob, but Israel, because you have struggled with God and with humans and have overcome."

GENESIS 32:28

E ventually Jacob would leave Laban's house. With his two wives, children, servants, and lots of cattle, goats, and sheep, he set out toward home. One night he had an encounter with the Lord that would change him for the better. It was like a new beginning, a fresh start for Jacob.

Jacob crossed the river. Just like he met God when he was leaving home, he would meet God again on his way back home. All alone. With no distractions. With no one to help him. Just him and the Lord.

"So Jacob was left alone, and a man wrestled with him till daybreak" (Genesis 32:24).

The first time God had come to him in a dream. This time it was in a wrestling match. Jacob would not give up. He struggled with God, wanting God to bless him just as He had promised. Finally, in the early hours of the morning, the Lord let Jacob go and asked him, "What is your name?"

He was about to give Jacob a new name. This was God's way of giving

KEY IDEA

God blesses with new beginnings. God would bless Jacob just as He promised. But He wanted Jacob to learn to surrender and let Him lead him. Jacob was a new man, with a new name and a new beginning.

Jacob a fresh start. God wanted Jacob to come home a different man from when he left home. The Lord gave Jacob the name *Israel*, which means "one who struggled with God." His descendants would eventually become the nation of Israel, the Israelites.

God touched Jacob's hip, causing him to walk with a limp. He was weakened by God in order to be strengthened by Him. Just like Jacob, we need to learn to surrender to God. To walk humbly with Him. To be the kind of people God wants us to be. And always remember that the Lord is the God of new beginnings and fresh starts!

LET'S DISCUSS TOGETHER

- *Why is it important to be alone with God?*
- *What did Jacob learn by wrestling with God?*
- *Why did God give Jacob a limp (Genesis 32:25)?*

LET'S PRAY TOGETHER

Lord, teach us to surrender to You. Thank You that You are full of love and grace. You are the God who gives new beginnings and fresh starts. You don't give up on us when we fail or sin. Continue to change us into the people You want us to be. In Jesus' name, amen.

● ● ● ● ● ● ● ●

For Further Study: Genesis 32:22-32

17

WITH A NEW FUTURE, JACOB FACES HIS PAST

• • • • • • • • •

Esau ran to meet Jacob and embraced him; he threw his arms
around his neck and kissed him. And they wept.

GENESIS 33:4

After a long night of wrestling with God, Jacob was ready to continue his journey. He had a new name, a new relationship with the
Lord, and a fresh start. But with a new future ahead of him, it was time
to confront his past—his relationship with his brother, Esau.

As Jacob and his family were getting ready to set out on their journey, he looked up and saw Esau coming toward him. That's not all. Esau
was not alone. Far from it. He had four hundred men with him!

Jacob, who had deceived his brother in the past, was terrified. He
must have thought, *Is my brother still mad? Does he still want to harm
me? Why all these men?* So Jacob split up his family, dividing them into
different camps.

He put his female servants and their children in the front. Leah and
her children were next in line. And then Rachel and her son, Joseph, were
in the back.

But then something unexpected happened, something Jacob didn't
see coming. Esau began to run . . . not to hurt Jacob but to hug him! "Esau

ran to meet Jacob and embraced him; he threw his arms around his neck and kissed him. And they wept" (Genesis 33:4).

They were putting their past behind them. Two brothers who had become enemies were now brothers again!

Change comes slowly for each of us. Our past doesn't have to follow us into the future. As God is at work in the world, He is changing us and making us new, one step at a time.

LET'S DISCUSS TOGETHER

- *Why did Jacob split up his family?*
- *Why do you think this showed a lack of trust in God?*
- *Why is forgiveness so important?*

LET'S PRAY TOGETHER

Father, thank You for being faithful and good to us. Thanks for the love and forgiveness You offer us through Jesus. Show us how to love one another in the same way You love us. In Jesus' name, amen.

• • • • • • •

For Further Study: Genesis 33:1–11

18

JOSEPH AND HIS DREAMS

• • • • • • • • •

When his brothers saw that their father loved him more than any of
them, they hated him and could not speak a kind word to him.

GENESIS 37:4

Sometimes following God is hard. Trials come our way. Our faith gets
tested. We are tempted to wonder what God is doing. This was especially true for one of Jacob's sons—Joseph.

Jacob loved Joseph more than any of his other sons. He loved him so
much that he made a beautiful and colorful robe just for him. God had
given Joseph several dreams. Dreams about how God was going to use
him to show the world what the Lord is like.

"We were out binding sheaves of grain in the field," Joseph explained
to his brothers, "and your sheaves bowed down to mine." That wasn't the
only dream. "I saw the sun and moon and eleven stars bowing down to
me," Joseph declared to his brothers.

One day Jacob sent Joseph to check on his brothers while they were
out in the field. Still angry and jealous over his dreams, the brothers
came up with a plan. They stripped Joseph of his coat, threw him into a
pit, and then sold him to some traders who were on their way to Egypt. If
that wasn't bad enough, they took Joseph's coat to their father, hoping he
would believe a wild animal had attacked Joseph and killed him.

Joseph's brothers had a plan—a bad plan—but God had a greater plan. Even though Joseph didn't understand it at the time, God was at work.

God knows what He is doing. Our job is to trust Him, even when it's hard. We too can be sure that when things seem out of control, God is still in control.

KEY IDEA

God uses hard stuff.
God often allows trials or tough times to accomplish His purposes. We might not always understand it. We might not always like it. But God is always in control, doing what is best. As we'll see, God was using some pretty hard things in Joseph's life to get him exactly where He wanted him.

LET'S DISCUSS TOGETHER

- *What do you think Joseph's dreams meant?*
- *Why do you think Joseph may have doubted his dreams after he was sold to traders?*
- *What is important for us to remember about God when we are going through a tough time?*

LET'S PRAY TOGETHER

Father, You never leave us or forget about us. You are always working out Your plans and purposes, even when life is hard. You are always in control. We love You and trust You. In Jesus' name, amen.

• • • • • •

For Further Study: Genesis 37

45

19

JOSEPH STANDS STRONG

• • • • • • • • •

How then could I do such a wicked thing and sin against God?
GENESIS 39:9

Has someone ever accused you of doing something you didn't do? How did it make you feel? Joseph had already been rejected by his brothers. Dumped in a pit. Then sold to traders heading to Egypt. What else could go wrong? As it turns out, a lot!

Potiphar, a very important Egyptian in charge of Pharaoh's army, bought Joseph from the traders. He took him to his big, expensive palace. He put him in charge of everything! God blessed Joseph. And God blessed everything Potiphar had.

But then one day while Potiphar was at work, Potiphar's wife kept asking Joseph to come with her. Joseph refused. He knew it wasn't right to go anywhere with Potiphar's wife. Day after day, she called to him. He kept saying, "No!" And he stood strong.

This made Potiphar's wife mad, so mad that she eventually made up a story about Joseph. She tried to make him look like a bad guy. It worked too. Potiphar had Joseph thrown into prison with the rest of the king's prisoners. Things were going from bad to worse! One thing didn't change though—Joseph refused to sin against God. No matter what.

Joseph was more concerned about pleasing God—no matter who

was watching. Joseph's love for God helped him live for God!

Joining God's work in the world can be hard. We have to stand out. Stand up. Stay strong. And never give in! God is still looking for people who love Him and will live for Him. With God's help, how will you stand strong?

LET'S DISCUSS TOGETHER

- *When have you ever been tempted to do something you knew wasn't right?*
- *How did Joseph's love for God help him live for God?*
- *Why is it always better to please God instead of pleasing people?*

LET'S PRAY TOGETHER

Lord, we praise You for always being with us. You are faithful and good. Give us power to stand strong for You. Help us say no to sin and yes to You. In Jesus' name, amen.

• • • • • • •

For Further Study: Genesis 39

20

FROM THE PALACE TO THE PRISON

• • • • • • • • •

While Joseph was there in the prison, the LORD was with him; he showed him kindness and granted him favor in the eyes of the prison warden.

GENESIS 39:20–21

W hen Joseph went from living in the palace to living in a prison, God never left him. God was still with him and working through him.

God gave Joseph favor. Just as he had been in charge of the palace, Joseph was soon put in charge of the prison. One day Joseph noticed two prisoners: one was the chief cupbearer and the other was the chief baker. "What's wrong?" he asked. They were confused about their dreams.

Joseph listened. Then he broke the news. It was good news for the cupbearer. "Pharaoh will set you free in three days, and you will return to your job!" Joseph said. But it was bad news for the baker. He would be punished in three days. Sure enough, the cupbearer was set free.

It would be several years before the cupbearer would remember Joseph. This time, it wasn't a prisoner who needed his help; it was Pharaoh himself! Joseph explained the dream—it was about seven years with lots of food and seven years with no food. Pharaoh was so impressed with Joseph that he put him in charge of everything in Egypt.

From a dream to a pit to a palace to a prison and then to a palace again, God was with Joseph (Genesis 39:3, 21). Even when we don't see God or understand what He is doing, He is working in us and through us!

LET'S DISCUSS TOGETHER

- *Describe a time when you wondered what God was doing.*
- *What doubts do you think Joseph had about God when he was in prison?*
- *How did the Lord show His love for Joseph in prison?*

LET'S PRAY TOGETHER

Lord, we don't always understand what You are doing or why You are doing it. But we can trust Your heart. We know You are good. We can trust Your promises. We know You are faithful. Help us honor You above all else. In Jesus' name, amen.

• • • • • • •

For Further Study: Genesis 40-41

21

JOSEPH AND HIS BROTHERS MEET AGAIN

• • • • • • • • •

Joseph said to them, "Don't be afraid. Am I in the place of God? You intended to harm me, but God intended it for good to accomplish what is now being done, the saving of many lives."

GENESIS 50:19-20

Little did Joseph know that God had placed him in Egypt for a very special reason at a very significant time.

There had been seven really good years, when Joseph wisely helped Egypt store up lots of grain for food. Then came seven really bad years. There was a famine in the land, and people were coming from all over to buy grain—including Joseph's family.

When Joseph's brother arrived from Canaan, Joseph spotted them. After all those years, there they were, right in front of him. Joseph knew who they were, but his brothers didn't recognize him. They bowed down to him. He tested them, asking them questions. But didn't tell them who he was quite yet.

When he couldn't take it any longer, he shouted, "I am Joseph, your brother!" His brothers were terrified, thinking he was going to punish them. And then he did something they really didn't expect. He told them it was God who sent him to Egypt to save many lives, including their own. God turned their evil into good. Joseph's brothers found a lot more than food; they found forgiveness!

Food or no food, God was still faithful. Jacob and his whole family moved to Egypt, where they and their descendants lived as one family again for nearly four hundred years. Just as He did then, God still takes the bad and turns it into good for His purposes.

LET'S DISCUSS TOGETHER

- *Why is it so hard to forgive?*
- *How did God turn evil into good?*
- *What does this story tell us about God's faithfulness?*

LET'S PRAY TOGETHER

Father, thank You that You are a God of forgiveness. You have taken away our sin by our faith in Jesus. Remind us that You are always at work, in the good and in the bad. We love You and trust You. In Jesus' name, amen.

• • • • • • •

For Further Study: Genesis 45

22

GOD DOES NOT FORGET

• • • • • • • • •

When the child grew older, she took him to Pharaoh's daughter and he became her son. She named him Moses, saying, "I drew him out of the water."

EXODUS 2:10

W here did I put my homework? Has anyone seen my lunch? I can't figure out what I did with my soccer cleats." Have you ever felt forgetful? As God continues His work in the world, one of the things we learn is that God does not forget. He always remembers His people.

Many years later Joseph and his brothers passed away. But the rest of their family grew bigger and bigger. Their faith would be tested when a new king in Egypt began to mistreat them, making them slaves.

This new king made a new rule, a really evil rule: all baby girls were allowed to live, but not the boys. "Every Hebrew boy that is born you must throw into the Nile, but let every girl live" (Exodus 1:22).

One mother feared God more than the king though. When she gave birth, she hid her son. Instead of throwing him in the river to die, she carefully placed him in a basket in the Nile River—to live. Guess who else was not far down the river? Pharaoh's daughter, who was bathing. When she saw the baby, she felt sorry for him, pulling him out of danger. She adopted him. And she gave him the name Moses, which means "I drew him out of the water."

God had a pretty big plan for Moses to lead the Israelites. No king was going to get in the way of the real King's work in the world! God didn't forget His people. He doesn't forget you. He knows you, loves you, and has promised to be with you, no matter what.

LET'S DISCUSS TOGETHER

- *What does it mean to fear God?*
- *How can fearing God help us fear people less?*
- *What do you learn about Moses' mom's faith?*

LET'S PRAY TOGETHER

Lord, You are like a Father and Friend to us. But You are also the King of kings. Your plans always prevail. Thank You that You never leave us. You don't forget us. And You are always at work, when things are going well and when things seem scary. In Jesus' name, amen.

● ● ● ● ● ● ●

For Further Study: Exodus 1; 2:1–10

23

GOD TELLS US HIS NAME

• • • • • • • • •

God said to Moses, "I AM WHO I AM. This is what you are to say to the
Israelites: 'I AM has sent me to you.'"

EXODUS 3:14

D o you know what your name means? Are you named after someone
in your family? There is a lot in a name—especially in God's name.

Moses may have grown up in Pharaoh's palace, but he was not going
to stay in Pharaoh's palace. His King was the God of Abraham, Isaac, and
Jacob, the God who was on the move, doing a great work in the world.

The Egyptians mistreated God's people. They were harsh. Cruel.
Unfair. As Moses grew up, he grew more upset at the way God's people
were being mistreated. In anger, he killed an Egyptian who was hurting
an Israelite. Knowing what he did was wrong, he fled to the desert.

But he was not alone for long. One day he encountered a bush. And it
was not just any bush. It was a bush on fire. And then, out of the flames,
he heard a voice—God's voice.

"Moses, Moses, you are on holy ground. Take off your sandals. I am
sending you back to Egypt to set my people free."

Then God told him His name. "Tell them I AM has sent you." When
God told Moses His name, He was really telling him who He is and what

He does. His name is His character. He is eternal, devoted to His people, compassionate, and powerful.

God still wants others to know His name—to know who He really is and what He has done for us. And guess what? He wants to work through *you* just as He did through Moses. It might be in your family. It could be in your school, your neighborhood, or even your church. So go—let someone know what God is really like!

LET'S DISCUSS TOGETHER

- *What does it say about God that He heard His people's cry?*
- *How does knowing God's name help us trust Him?*
- *What is one way we can let other people know what God is really like?*

LET'S PRAY TOGETHER

God, thank You for telling us who You are. Because we know Your name, we can trust You and rely on You. You are full of power. You are faithful to us. And You always treat us better than we deserve. In Jesus' name, amen.

● ● ● ● ● ● ●

For Further Study: Exodus 3

24

NO ONE LIKE OUR GOD

• • • • • • • • •

I will take you as my own people, and I will be your God. Then you
will know that I am the LORD your God, who brought you out from
under the yoke of the Egyptians.

EXODUS 6:7

Who is the most powerful person you know? The Israelites had
been slaves in Egypt for a long time, but things were about to
change. God was about to save them by setting them free.

Back to Egypt Moses went. And along with him went his brother,
Aaron. Over and over again they told Pharaoh what God had told them
to say: "Let My people go!" But Pharaoh wouldn't. His heart was hard,
and he refused to listen to God.

So God did something out of the ordinary. He performed many different miracles to show His love and power. The Bible calls these miracles
plagues. There were ten, to be exact.

God turned all the water in Egypt to blood. Then He sent frogs,
hopping and jumping, everywhere. Then gnats. Flies. All the Egyptians'
cattle died. Painful sores called boils covered their skin. Hail pounded
the earth. Locusts swarmed everywhere. Darkness fell on them like a
blanket.

And finally, the worst plague of all: every firstborn male died unless they had put the blood of a lamb around their door.

KEY IDEA

God alone is to be loved and served. God showed His people that He is greater and stronger than the gods of Egypt. There is no one like our God!

But God never punishes sin without offering to pay for our sin. God promised to "pass over" the houses that were covered in the blood of a lamb. Sadly, the Egyptians rejected God's love and offer to be saved.

Later in the Bible, Jesus is called our Passover Lamb. He died for us on the cross. His blood covers us. And guess what? When we put our faith in Jesus, God saves us and sets us free from our sin.

LET'S DISCUSS TOGETHER

- *Why did Pharaoh not listen to God?*
- *How did God show His power?*
- *What does this story tell us about Jesus?*

LET'S PRAY TOGETHER

God, there is no one like You. Help us keep You number one in our lives. Thank You for saving us, forgiving us, and setting us free to love and serve You. In Jesus' name, amen.

● ● ● ● ● ● ●

For Further Study: Exodus 5–12

57

25

GOD ALWAYS PROVIDES

• • • • • • • • •

I will sing to the LORD, for he is highly exalted. Both horse and driver
he has hurled into the sea.

EXODUS 15:1

Egypt was not going to give up without a fight. Pharaoh gathered his
army, loaded up his chariots, and began to chase his former slaves.
The Israelites were stuck. Egypt's army was behind them; the Red Sea
was in front of them.

But God had His people right where He wanted them. They had no
choice but to depend on Him. "Watch," Moses said: "The LORD will fight
for you; you need only to be still" (Exodus 14:14).

And sure enough, as Moses stretched out his hand, the wall of water
before them split in two. Thousands and thousands of Israelites marched
across the sea on dry ground. The Egyptians? They weren't so lucky. Just
as quickly as God parted the waters, He gathered them. The sea swallowed them.

Every chariot.

Every weapon.

Every soldier.

God had fought for the Israelites, and they couldn't help but
praise Him!

But it wouldn't take long for God's people to forget God's power. They had a long journey ahead of them as they traveled toward the land God had promised. The desert was very different from Egypt. It was hot, full of rocks and sand and mountains. There were wild animals. Danger lurked at every turn.

They grew hungry, thirsty, and even angry, wanting to go back to Egypt. But God provided everything they needed. He gave them birds to eat, called quail. He rained down bread from heaven that they called manna. And He even brought forth water from a rock.

God is still fighting for His people. His power works in us and through us. Just like the Israelites, we have to learn to trust God if we are going to live for Him.

LET'S DISCUSS TOGETHER

- *When have we seen God provide for our family?*
- *Why doesn't God like complaining?*
- *How do you need to trust God right now?*

LET'S PRAY TOGETHER

We praise You, God, for You are on our side. You fight for us. You always provide what we need. And You have promised never to leave us. In Jesus' name, amen.

● ● ● ● ● ● ●

For Further Study: Exodus 14–17

60

26

A NEW WAY TO LIVE

• • • • • • • • •

Oh, how I love your law! I meditate on it all day long.

PSALM 119:97

Have you ever had friends tell you something about themselves? God, who is like a Father and Friend to us, has revealed Himself to us in the Bible. He doesn't want us to guess who He is.

The Israelites had a long journey ahead of them to the promised land. God's goal wasn't just travel; it was transformation. One of the ways He was going to change His people was by communicating with them. He was going to tell them more about who He is and how He wanted them to live.

One day as the Israelites were camped in the desert, He told them to get ready. He was going to come down to the mountain and give Moses instructions for living. Exodus 19:20 says, "The LORD descended to the top of Mount Sinai and called Moses to the top of the mountain. So Moses went up."

There was lightning. Thunder. A thick cloud. Even the sound of loud trumpet blasts. God spoke while the people shook with fear.

On two stone tables, God gave Moses the Ten Commandments:

Keep God as your only god.

Don't worship anything but God.

Honor God's name.

Keep the Sabbath day by resting and not doing any work.

Honor your parents.

Do not murder.

Always love your spouse.

Do not steal.

Do not lie.

Do not want what others have.

God was showing His people how to live, how to be a different kind of people who would show the world what He is like. He was also showing them how to have real joy, peace, and freedom.

Real happiness is not found in doing whatever we want. Real happiness is found in doing what God wants.

LET'S DISCUSS TOGETHER

- *Why do you think God told the Israelites not to touch the mountain?*
- *Why is it important to know God's Word?*
- *How do our actions tell others about who God is?*

LET'S PRAY TOGETHER

God, thank You for telling us what You are like. We love Your Word.
Continue to teach us and help us always obey You in all that we do,
say, and think. In Jesus' name, amen.

● ● ● ● ● ● ●

For Further Study: Exodus 19–20

27

THE ISRAELITES TURN AWAY FROM GOD

• • • • • • • • •

The LORD relented and did not bring on his people the disaster he had threatened.

EXODUS 32:14

W hen was the last time you made a mistake? How did you try to correct it? As God continues to reveal Himself, we discover that He is far more faithful than we are. He is completely without sin. But He is also forgiving.

The Israelites had just witnessed God's amazing power and love in action. But then they did the unthinkable. Because Moses was taking so long coming down from the mountain, they asked Aaron to make them another god.

Instead of choosing to lead the Israelites out of sin, Aaron led them right into sin! He collected all their gold jewelry, melted it down, and shaped it into a big golden calf. Then they threw a party. All the Israelites danced and sang, worshipping a lie instead of worshipping the Lord.

Because God is holy, He became angry at their sin. Moses prayed and pleaded with God to forgive His people.

Even though God had to punish their sin, He never stopped loving them. The Israelites had made a huge mistake! But He forgave them. And the work God was doing in the world continued, even though God's people weren't always perfect.

The Israelites were quick to forget who God is and all He had done for them. They stopped trusting Him and turned from Him. But God didn't give up on them. And He doesn't give up on us when we sin. Even when we are forgetful or unfaithful, God is still forgiving when we turn back to Him.

KEY IDEA

We need a mediator. A mediator is someone who goes between us and someone else to make peace; Moses did that with God for the Israelites. The Bible says that Jesus is our final and perfect Mediator (1 Timothy 2:5) because of what He did for us on the cross.

LET'S DISCUSS TOGETHER

- *Why did the Israelites forget God?*
- *What should we do when we sin against God?*
- *Why is it encouraging that God works through imperfect people?*

LET'S PRAY TOGETHER

Father, we praise You because You are full of grace. You treat us better than we deserve. Forgive us when we sin, and remind us of what Jesus has done for us on the cross. In Jesus' name, amen.

● ● ● ● ● ● ●

For Further Study: Exodus 32

28

GOD LIVES WITH HIS PEOPLE

• • • • • • • • •

The cloud covered the tent of meeting, and the glory of the Lord
filled the tabernacle.

EXODUS 40:34

God used to live with His people, Adam and Eve, in the perfect
place, the garden of Eden. All that changed, though, when their
sin separated them from their Father and Friend.

Of course, God never left the people He loved. He had been with
Noah. He appeared to Abram. He was faithful to Isaac and Jacob. He
rescued Moses. He delivered the Israelites. But now, He was going to
live among them. He was going to go with them on their journey to the
promised land.

God loves to be close to His people—which is why He gave so many
important instructions to the Israelites about making a place for Him
to live among them. This place would be in a tent called the tabernacle.

It wasn't that God needed a place to live; it was that God's people
needed a place to worship—a place to meet with God. They needed a
place where they could come to Him the right way for friendship. So
Moses recorded God's instructions for every detail about how to build
the tabernacle, especially the different instructions about which sacri-
fices and offerings they were to bring to the priests.

And then the Bible says God's presence and His glory filled the tabernacle. A cloud covered it when God wanted them to stay, and it moved when God was telling them to go. God lived among His people! Every step of the way, He was leading them. Aren't you glad that God is still with us today, loving us and leading us in all we do?

KEY IDEA

God wants us to worship Him His way. God lived among His people and gave them instructions for how to have a relationship with Him. The Israelites weren't free to come to Him their way but God's way!

LET'S DISCUSS TOGETHER

- *Why is it important to come to God His way?*
- *What does it say about God that He wanted to live among His people?*
- *How does God live among us today?*

LET'S PRAY TOGETHER

Lord, we praise You and thank You that You are always with us. You never leave us or forsake us. And we praise You because You have made a way for us to have a relationship with You through our faith in Jesus. In Jesus' name, amen.

● ● ● ● ● ● ●

For Further Study: Exodus 40

29

WHEN A JOB SEEMS TOO BIG (AND SCARY)

• • • • • • • • •

Do not rebel against the LORD. And do not be afraid of the people of the land, because we will devour them. Their protection is gone, but the LORD is with us. Do not be afraid of them.

NUMBERS 14:9

Have you ever been asked to do something that seemed too hard? Or too scary? Well, the Israelites were just about ready to enter the promised land called Canaan. The problem was that there were already people living in the land—people who didn't like God or the Israelites.

So Moses sent out twelve spies to explore the land of Canaan. "See what the people are like," he said. "Find out if they are weak or strong. Check out their towns. Inspect the land. And bring back some fruit while you are at it!"

For forty days and forty nights, the spies did as they were told. When they returned, they gave their report. A bad report. A report that spread fear among God's people.

"The people are huge. Too strong for us. And the towns are well protected. We can't enter the land," they said. Not all of the spies agreed though. Caleb and Joshua spoke up, silencing the other men. With great courage and faith, they said, "The Lord is with us. He will fight for us and protect us. Don't rebel against the Lord!"

And God was pleased with their faith. So pleased that only Caleb and Joshua, along with the next generation of Israel, would enter the land. Even when something seems too hard or too scary or if we stand alone, God is always pleased by our faith and trust in Him.

LET'S DISCUSS TOGETHER

- *Why were Caleb and Joshua so confident?*
- *How can our faith inspire or help others?*
- *How does God reward our faith?*

KEY IDEA

Faith is confidence in what we do not see. Real faith is trust in God that leads to action for God. Caleb and Joshua saw the same things the spies did. But the difference was that they saw God differently. They trusted that He really was with them and was good and powerful.

LET'S PRAY TOGETHER

Lord, we trust You. Even when things around us might be hard or scary, we know You are with us. So help us listen to You, love You, and obey You. Our faith is in You alone. In Jesus' name, amen.

● ● ● ● ● ● ●

For Further Study: Numbers 13–14

30

GOD WELCOMES ALL

• • • • • • • • •

Now then, please swear to me by the LORD that you will show
kindness to my family, because I have shown kindness to you.
JOSHUA 2:12

God does not love just some people and not others. That's what one
woman named Rahab who was not an Israelite discovered when
two strangers showed up at her door.

Joshua had taken over as the leader of the Israelites after Moses
died. As they were preparing to enter the promised land and attack a
city called Jericho, Joshua sent out two spies. Where did they go first? To
Rahab's house.

Not only was Rahab not an Israelite, but she had a bad reputation for
being pretty sinful too. When the king of Jericho sent a message to her
looking for the spies, she told him they had escaped, but really she had
hidden them on her roof.

She said to the spies, "We've heard about all the Lord has done for
you, and our hearts are melting with fear." Even though Rahab didn't
know everything about God, she knew enough to trust Him. She promised to hide the spies if they promised to protect her and her family when
the Israelites attacked.

"Tie this scarlet rope in your window. Make sure your entire family is with you in your home," they told her. "Then when Jericho is destroyed, you and your family will be saved."

Sure enough, when the Israelites attacked, God protected Rahab and saved her. The walls of Jericho fell, but Rahab's faith stood strong. Her story reminds us that there is no one outside of God's love. No one too far away or too sinful. And do you know what is even more surprising? Rahab eventually became the great-great-grandmother of King David. It was from her family that Jesus would eventually come!

KEY IDEA

God loves everyone. God chose Israel to tell the world what He is like, but God's love is for everyone. By faith, we have to choose to accept God's love and forgiveness.

LET'S DISCUSS TOGETHER

- *How did Rahab show her faith?*
- *What does this story tell us about God's love?*
- *What does this tell us about how we should love others?*

LET'S PRAY TOGETHER

Father, thank You for loving us no matter what. You are patient and full of compassion, always willing to forgive. Teach us to love others in the same way You love us. In Jesus' name, amen.

● ● ● ● ● ● ●

For Further Study: Joshua 2

31

GOD KEEPS HIS PROMISES

• • • • • • • • •

You know with all your heart and soul that not one of all the good promises the LORD your God gave you has failed. Every promise has been fulfilled; not one has failed.

JOSHUA 23:14

Has someone ever made you a promise? Did they do what they said they were going to do? When Joshua was very old, he wanted to remind the Israelites about something very important—God's promises.

The Bible is full of promises. They are important and powerful promises. Full of hope. Words of assurance. Reminders of victory. Encouragement to keep going.

Like a good Father, God is faithful, powerful, and loving. He is a Friend who watches over us and takes care of us. He is a promise maker, and He is also a promise keeper. God always follows through on what He says He is going to do.

This is exactly what Joshua wanted God's people to know and believe. Shortly before he died, Joshua held a big gathering. He called all the elders, leaders, judges, and people of Israel together. He knew how easy it would be to forget about God now that they were living in the promised land. He wanted them to renew their commitment to always love and serve God.

More than anything, Joshua wanted the Israelites to remember they were a part of a very special work in the world that God was doing through them. As God's people, they were like a light to all the other nations around them. But they would need to stay close to God. Listen to Him. Obey Him. And always trust that what God says, God will do!

In life, we need promises. Even as Christians, we encounter many different joys and sorrows. But we never go through life without the promise that God is with us and for us.

KEY IDEA

God is faithful. The Israelites were renewing their commitment to keep their covenant with God. Just like us, they needed the reminder that God is faithful—He always does what He says He is going to do.

LET'S DISCUSS TOGETHER

- *Why do we need to remember God's promises?*
- *Why is it hard sometimes to believe God's promises?*
- *What is one promise you need to remember right now, and why?*

LET'S PRAY TOGETHER

Father, You are good. You love us far more than we can love You. Be close to us. Always keep Your word to us. We know and trust that You are faithful. In Jesus' name, amen.

● ● ● ● ● ●

For Further Study: Joshua 23

32

GOD WORKS THROUGH THE WEAK

• • • • • • • • •

The LORD turned to him and said, "Go in the strength you have and save Israel out of Midian's hand. Am I not sending you?" "Pardon me, my lord," Gideon replied, "but how can I save Israel? My clan is the weakest in Manasseh, and I am the least in my family."

JUDGES 6:14–15

Not long after Joshua died, the Israelites turned to other gods. They didn't keep their promise to the greatest promise keeper ever! But God's work in the world didn't stop. God didn't give up. He raised up leaders, called judges, of Israel.

The Israelites would follow God, and then they would forget about God. This cycle went on and on. Each time when God's people would cry out for help, God would send a judge to bring God's people back to Himself.

One judge came from a small family. His name was Gideon. And Gideon felt too weak to be a part of God's work in the world. But God was not worried!

Even after Gideon gathered together thousands and thousands of soldiers, God told him to take only three hundred men into battle against the Midianites. It was God's strength, not theirs, that would win the battle!

"Surround the Midianites at night," God said. "Take torches and swords, and when the time is right, make lots of noise by smashing your clay jars." Gideon and the Israelites did just as God had said. And sure enough, it worked! The Midianites were defeated.

Have you ever felt too young or too small to be used by God? So did Gideon! His story reminds us that God's strength is at work in us and through us. God does His greatest work through the weak.

KEY IDEA

God uses the weak in His work. We don't have to feel strong to be used by God. We don't even have to know everything about the Bible or God. We just have to step out in faith and trust God with the results!

LET'S DISCUSS TOGETHER

- *Why did God tell Gideon to send so many soldiers home?*
- *Why do you think God uses the weak?*
- *How can you be a part of God's work in your neighborhood or school?*

LET'S PRAY TOGETHER

Lord, work through us. Take the gifts we have and use them in Your work in the world. Help us be brave and trust You as we step out in faith to follow You. In Jesus' name, amen.

• • • • • • •

For Further Study: Judges 6-7

33

THE REAL SOURCE OF SAMSON'S STRENGTH

• • • • • • • • •

The woman gave birth to a boy and named him Samson. He grew
and the Lord blessed him, and the Spirit of the LORD began to stir
him while he was in Mahaneh Dan, between Zorah and Eshtaol.

JUDGES 13:24–25

Once again the Israelites had turned to idols. God was about to use
another unlikely person. His name was Samson.

The Lord blessed Samson, and the Spirit of God was with him. As
Samson grew up, he also grew stronger. He had not only the kind of
strength you need to lift heavy weights or break large objects, but the
kind of strength you need to live for God.

Samson did many great things. He fought and defeated thirty soldiers. He caught three hundred foxes, tied them tail to tail, and used
them to destroy the Philistines' fields. One day when Samson was about
to be handed over to the Philistines, God's power helped him break free
and strike down one thousand soldiers with the jawbone of a donkey!

But Samson didn't always trust God. He married a Philistine woman,
and later he fell in love with a woman named Delilah. The Philistines
wanted Delilah to help discover the secret of Samson's strength.

After tricking her several times, Samson finally told her: "No razor
has ever been used on my head," he said, "because I have been a Nazirite

dedicated to God from my mother's womb. If my head were shaved, my strength would leave me, and I would become as weak as any other man."

That night Delilah had Samson's head shaved. He was captured and blinded by the Philistines. He had lost his strength from the Lord because he had strayed from Him. But at a feast for the Philistines' false god, Dagon, God gave Samson strength one last time to defeat them.

We need to stay close to God. We need to trust Him. And always remember that's it's not our strength but God's strength at work in us!

LET'S DISCUSS TOGETHER

- *How did Samson stray from God?*
- *What was the real source of his strength?*
- *What do we need God's strength for today?*

LET'S PRAY TOGETHER

Lord, give us the power we need to live for You each day. Help us be set apart for You, pleasing You in everything we do. In Jesus' name, amen.

● ● ● ● ● ●

For Further Study: Judges 13–16

34

GIVE US A KING!

• • • • • • • • •

The people refused to listen to Samuel. "No!" they said. "We want
a king over us. Then we will be like all the other nations, with a king
to lead us and to go out before us and fight our battles."

1 SAMUEL 8:19-20

Do you know someone who is always getting in trouble? The
Israelites were a lot like that! They were always turning to God
then turning away. Over and over again, they seemed to love God one
minute then leave Him the next.

But God was always gracious, treating them far better than they
deserved! He had always been their King. He led them through Moses
then Joshua. When the Israelites settled into the promised land, they had
judges. Each step of the way, God was with them and for them—loyal
with His love and quick to forgive.

But soon God's people noticed something. There was something different about their neighbors. They had a king, but Israel didn't.

"Give us a king," they complained to Samuel, who was one of God's
prophets. "All our neighbors have kings to lead them. They have kings
who fight for them. We want a king like that!"

This saddened the Lord. He said to Samuel, "It is not you they have
rejected, but they have rejected Me as their king." So the Lord gave them

their first king, Saul. He too, like Israel, was not always faithful. And so God didn't let him be king for long.

If we are honest, we can be a lot like the Israelites who didn't want God to rule them. Sometimes we too can reject God as our good and loving King.

LET'S DISCUSS TOGETHER

- *Why did the Israelites reject God as their King?*
- *How should a good king rule his people?*
- *How do we let God rule our lives today?*

KEY IDEA

Jesus is the real King. As we'll see, God will promise to send the real King to lead His people. He will be a Savior who will die for the sins of His people. But He will also be a good King who will lead God's people back to living for God's purposes in the world.

LET'S PRAY TOGETHER

Jesus, You are our King. We want to do what You want, not just what we want. Lead us and help us to be the people You want us to be. In Jesus' name, amen.

● ● ● ● ● ● ●

For Further Study: 1 Samuel 8

79

35

DAVID, GOD'S NEW CHOSEN KING

• • • • • • • • •

The LORD said to Samuel, "Do not consider his appearance or his height, for I have rejected him. The LORD does not look at the things people look at. People look at the outward appearance, but the LORD looks at the heart."

1 SAMUEL 16:7

W hat do you notice about people when you first meet them? Is it their hair? How about their clothes? Maybe you notice whether they are tall or short. When God rejected Saul as king of Israel, He replaced him with David. But when people first looked at David, they didn't notice that he was very kinglike.

The Lord told Samuel to go to the house of Jesse, a man who lived in a tiny little town called Bethlehem. He said, "I have chosen one of Jesse's sons to be king." Jesse had a lot of sons. One by one, he brought them out. God kept saying, "Nope, not that one! No, no, and no, not that one either!"

Finally, Samuel asked Jesse, "Do you have any more sons?"

"I do," Jesse said. "He is the youngest of all my sons. But he is out watching our sheep." Jesse must have been thinking to himself, *Surely Samuel is not looking for David!*

But sure enough, that is exactly who the Lord had chosen as the next king of Israel. As soon as David came in from the field, the Lord said to Samuel, "He is the one. Anoint him with oil." And when he did, the Spirit of God came upon David. Soon he would be king.

God did not choose David because he was tall or because he was strong or good-looking. God chose David because he had a heart for the Lord. What God notices is not how we look but what we love. People look at the outside, but God looks at the inside. He cares more about our hearts—whether we truly love Him or not.

LET'S DISCUSS TOGETHER

- *Why didn't Jesse call for David until last?*
- *What does it mean that God looks at our hearts?*
- *How can we see people the same way God does?*

LET'S PRAY TOGETHER

Jesus, You are our King. We want to do what You want, not just what we want. Lead us and help us be the people You want us to be. In Jesus' name, amen.

• • • • • •

For Further Study: 1 Samuel 16:1–13

36

DAVID AND GOLIATH

• • • • • • • • •

David said to Saul, "Let no one lose heart on account of this
Philistine; your servant will go and fight him."

1 SAMUEL 17:32

When have you ever been scared to do something? How did you
overcome your fear? David, who would later become king, was
no stranger to scary situations! Neither were the Israelites.

There they were, face-to-face with one of their worst enemies—the
Philistines. For forty days, Goliath, a giant soldier, heckled the Israelites.
He was dressed from head to toe in shiny armor. He had a sword, a jave-
lin, and a real appetite for fighting!

Goliath was so fierce that every single one of the Israelites was too
afraid to go out and fight him—except for one Israelite. David, the young
shepherd, was sent to the battlefield not to fight but to deliver some food.
All that changed when he heard what Goliath was yelling.

Saul tried to give young David his armor and sword, but David
refused. Instead, he marched in the direction of Goliath. He had heard
enough. What David did have was his faith, a slingshot, and a few stones.
David said to the Philistine, "You come against me with sword and spear
and javelin, but I come against you in the name of the LORD Almighty,
the God of the armies of Israel, whom you have defied" (1 Samuel 17:45).

He loaded his slingshot with a stone. Then he let it fly. The bigger the giant, the bigger the fall. Sure enough, when David's stone met Goliath's head, the giant crashed to the ground! Once again God had saved His people—and He did it through one faithful and courageous shepherd boy.

When we are living for God, it's not always easy. It takes courage and boldness. God always gives us His strength when we stand up and stand out for Him. Where do you need to be strong for God?

KEY IDEA

God uses what we have, not what we don't have. David had a slingshot and some stones. Each of us has different gifts or abilities that God can use for His glory.

LET'S DISCUSS TOGETHER

- *Why were the Israelites so afraid?*
- *What did David believe that the Israelites didn't?*
- *In what ways do you need to stand up for God?*

LET'S PRAY TOGETHER

Lord, give each of us courage to live for You. Help us not be afraid of what other people think of us. We want to love You and live for You. In Jesus' name, amen.

• • • • • • •

For Further Study: 1 Samuel 17

37

FRIENDS FOREVER

• • • • • • • • •

Jonathan had David reaffirm his oath out of love for him, because he loved him as he loved himself.

1 SAMUEL 20:17

W ho is your closest friend? What makes him or her a good friend? David was not yet king, but he quickly became a hero who, just like us, needed a good friend! He needed a friend who would stick with him and, most importantly, one who would join him in living and serving the Lord.

Young David had just returned from the battlefield. Goliath was dead. And now all Israel was singing his praises! First Samuel 18:6–7 says:

When the men were returning home after David had killed the Philistine, the women came out from all the towns of Israel to meet King Saul with singing and dancing, with joyful songs and with timbrels and lyres. As they danced, they sang: "Saul has slain his thousands, and David his tens of thousands."

King Saul was not happy. He became jealous of David. Saul kept a close eye on him. Eventually he became so mad that he even tried to kill David. But King Saul's son, Jonathan, would have no part in it!

He knew the Lord was with David. He knew God had chosen him to continue His work in the world. Instead of joining his dad, Jonathan joined David and became his closest friend. He loved him, protected him, and listened to him. Jonathan was always there to encourage David in his relationship with the Lord.

Do you have friends like Jonathan? As we join God's work in the world, we need the right kind of friends. Friends who are following God. Friends who are making us better, stronger, and more like Jesus. And we need to be that kind of friend to those around us too!

KEY IDEA

Who we hang out with today shapes who we become tomorrow. The Bible tells us to choose our friends wisely. Our friends affect how we act, what we think, and eventually who we become!

LET'S DISCUSS TOGETHER

- *What made Jonathan such a good friend?*
- *How do friends either hurt us or help us?*
- *What can you do to be a friend like Jonathan to others?*

LET'S PRAY TOGETHER

Father, thank You for being the best Friend of all. Give us wisdom to choose our friends wisely. Help us be the right kind of friend—a friend who loves, encourages, and points others to You. In Jesus' name, amen.

• • • • • • •

For Further Study: 1 Samuel 20

38

GOD'S PROMISE TO DAVID

• • • • • • • • •

He is the one who will build a house for my Name, and I will
establish the throne of his kingdom forever.

2 SAMUEL 7:13

Have you ever felt you had to earn someone's love? Why did you feel like that? We can never earn God's love, nor can we lose it. This is a lesson David learned when he eventually became king.

David was thirty years old when he finally became king. He had a heart devoted to God, a heart that wanted to please God more than anything! And David did a lot of good things for God and for God's people.

He made Israel one—bringing all the tribes together.

He crushed their enemies.

He made Jerusalem the capital city.

He brought the ark of the covenant there, the ark that held the two stone tablets God had given to Moses.

David even wanted to build a temple for the Lord.

As much as David loved God, he sinned against God too. But God never stopped loving him.

Here's the good news! It's not what David did for the Lord that mattered most. It's what the Lord did for David. What did He do? He made a promise that someone from his family would rule forever.

Though David didn't know it and wouldn't live long enough to see it, that someone would be Jesus! A King who would always do what was right. A King who would be like a shepherd—someone who would lead and protect God's people. And a King who would be a Savior, who would even give His life to save sinners like us!

As much as we love God, we need to remember that God loves us more. He gives us more than we deserve. He has done far more for us than we could ever do for Him!

LET'S DISCUSS TOGETHER

- *How does God love us more than we love Him?*
- *Why is it important to remember we can't earn God's love?*
- *What are you most thankful to God for?*

LET'S PRAY TOGETHER

Lord, You always treat us better than we deserve. Even when we sin, You love us and forgive us. Help us show our love for You by always trying to live for You. In Jesus' name, amen.

● ● ● ● ● ● ●

For Further Study: 2 Samuel 7

39

TAKING SIN SERIOUSLY

• • • • • • • •

Have mercy on me, O God, according to your unfailing love;
according to your great compassion blot out my transgressions.
Wash away all my iniquity and cleanse me from my sin.

PSALM 51:1-2

H as someone ever tricked you? Did they promise you something and then not follow through? Sin can work a lot like that. It might look good. It might seem like it would be fun. It's tempting. We think it might give us more happiness than loving God. But it never does!

Even King David was fooled by sin.

One day when his army was out to battle, he was roaming around on the roof of his palace when he noticed a woman. She was a very beautiful woman. Her name was Bathsheba. The problem was that Bathsheba was not David's wife!

Instead of running from sin, he ran right into it. He sent messengers to bring Bathsheba to his palace. He also planned to have Bathsheba's husband, Uriah, killed during battle. Before long, Bathsheba had a baby. And David had a big problem.

He couldn't hide his sin from others, especially not from God. And so the Lord sent the prophet Nathan to David. Like a good friend, Nathan told David the truth about his sin—that his sin was evil in God's eyes, it was hurting David, and it had hurt others. He also broke the news that Bathsheba's child would not live. David broke down because of his sin. He knew what he did was wrong.

Even though God is full of love and quick to forgive, sin is serious—it always steals the life God has for us. What God has for us is always better than what sin offers us. So be careful. Watch out—don't be tricked!

KEY IDEA

Sin is serious. While God forgives, there can be bad consequences for our sin. God is loving and always ready to forgive when we confess our sin to Him. But sin is serious to God. He knows how much it steals the life He wants for us.

LET'S DISCUSS TOGETHER

- *What should David have done?*
- *How can sin have consequences even when God forgives?*
- *What is one way to stay on guard against sin?*

LET'S PRAY TOGETHER

Father, protect us from sinning against You. Help us be wise, alert, and strong when we face temptation. In Jesus' name, amen.

• • • • • • •

For Further Study: 2 Samuel 11–12

40

ASKING FOR WISDOM

• • • • • • • • •

Give your servant a discerning heart to govern your people and to distinguish between right and wrong. For who is able to govern this great people of yours?

1 KINGS 3:9

Who is the smartest person you know? What makes him or her so smart? We aren't born with all the answers, are we? We have to learn. Ask for advice. Be teachable. Listen. And then live it out! This is exactly what the next king of Israel did.

Even though David wasn't perfect, he had a heart for God. The Lord worked through him in some pretty amazing ways. He didn't stop with David though. God continued His work through David's son, Solomon.

When Solomon became the king of Israel, he knew he needed some help. Lots of help! His father had taught him a lot about living for God, but not everything. And so when the Lord asked Solomon what he wanted more than anything, he answered, "Wisdom!"

Solomon could have asked for fame. Or he could have asked for money. The Lord gave him both. He even used him to build a huge and beautiful temple in Jerusalem. But the most important thing He gave Solomon was wisdom.

God gave Solomon the ability to know right from wrong, to be fair with the Israelites, and to make good decisions. He became so wise that people from other countries came to visit him and ask him questions.

As we partner with God in what He is doing in the world, we need wisdom too. Just like Solomon, we need to ask God for His truth. And guess what? God has promised to give us wisdom and knowledge when we seek Him in His Word. So don't be afraid to ask—God gives generously to those who want to know Him more!

KEY IDEA

Wisdom is knowing God's truth and living God's truth. It's not enough to have all the right answers. We need to live wisely too! One of the main ways God gives us wisdom is through the Bible. Read it, memorize it, and live it out. The world needs God's people who are walking in wisdom.

LET'S DISCUSS TOGETHER

- *What is wisdom?*
- *Why do we need wisdom so badly?*
- *How do we gain wisdom from God?*

LET'S PRAY TOGETHER

Father, give us wisdom. Teach us not only to know Your truth but also to live it out. Help us choose what is right and good, honoring You in all we do. In Jesus' name, amen.

● ● ● ● ● ● ●

For Further Study: 1 Kings 1–4

91

41

THINGS FALL APART

• • • • • • • • •

As Solomon grew old, his wives turned his heart after other gods,
and his heart was not fully devoted to the Lord his God, as the
heart of David his father had been.

1 KINGS 11:4

Have you ever started something but didn't finish it? Maybe you
started strong and then ran out of steam. Solomon's life is a good
example of starting well but not finishing well!

Solomon ruled over all Israel as king for forty years. Like his father
David, he loved God. At the beginning of his life, he wanted to live for
God and show others what God is really like. Things changed though. As
Solomon grew old, his heart grew cold.

He bought a great number of horses for himself and gathered lots of
gold and silver. Solomon didn't just marry one wife; he had seven hundred! Nor did he always treat God's people fairly. Solomon did evil in the
eyes of the Lord and didn't follow God with his whole heart.

And so God sent a messenger, a prophet, who declared that the kingdom would soon be divided. No longer would God's people be one—they
would be two. There would be a kingdom in the north called Israel and a
kingdom in the south called Judah. Sure enough, after Solomon died, his
son Rehoboam became king of Judah. Jeroboam became king of Israel.

Even though Solomon didn't finish well, God was still in charge. And even though each kingdom would have its own king—some would be good, but most of them bad—God would not lose control. He was still the real King, accomplishing His purposes through imperfect people.

LET'S DISCUSS TOGETHER

- *How did Solomon start well?*
- *Why did Solomon's love for God grow cold?*
- *Why is it important today to remember God is the real King who is in control?*

LET'S PRAY TOGETHER

Lord, You are King. Nothing surprises You, scares You, or is too hard for You. You even work through sinful rulers to accomplish Your work in the world. Help us trust You and always remember that You are good and strong. In Jesus' name, amen.

• • • • • • •

For Further Study: 1 Kings 11–14

42

WHO ALONE IS GOD?

• • • • • • • • •

Elijah went before the people and said, "How long will you waver between two opinions? If the LORD is God, follow him; but if Baal is God, follow him."

1 KINGS 18:21

God does not force us to love Him. We all have a choice. Will we serve Him or something else? This was the choice God's people had to make when King Ahab and his wife, Jezebel, were in charge in Israel.

God's people had been wavering back and forth. One minute they followed God; the next minute they followed an idol named Baal. So God sent His people a prophet named Elijah.

"Make up your mind," Elijah said. "Either the Lord really is God or not."

Elijah didn't stop there. He called everyone to the top of Mount Carmel—even the prophets of Baal. A showdown was about to happen. "Offer a sacrifice to your god," he said. "If he is real, he will send fire from heaven to burn up your offering."

Nothing happened. Not even a spark. And then Elijah placed an offering on the altar. To show that he was serious and that God was real, he even poured lots of water on the altar. Not just once—three times!

Fire, lots of fire, poured down from the sky. So much fire and heat that the entire altar was consumed—leaving everyone, including God's people, with a choice. Would they trust God and live for Him or not?

We might not worship a golden statue or wooden image. But anything that is more important to us than God, even good things, can be an idol. Each day we too have a choice. So who will you worship?

LET'S DISCUSS TOGETHER

- *How can something good take the place of God?*
- *What does it mean to truly worship God?*
- *How do people today go back and forth living for God?*

LET'S PRAY TOGETHER

Lord, You alone are worthy of our worship. Nothing can ever take Your place. Guard our hearts from making other things more important than You. Help us trust You each day, truly believing that living with You is better than anything else. In Jesus' name, amen.

● ● ● ● ● ● ●

For Further Study: 1 Kings 18

43

NEVER TOO FAR GONE FOR GOD

• • • • • • • • •

"Go to the great city of Nineveh and preach against it, because its wickedness has come up before me."

JONAH 1:2

D o you know someone who doesn't believe in God? Do you have a friend or family member you have invited to church, but they never want to come? The people living in Nineveh were a lot like that. They were not interested in knowing or loving God.

When the Lord told Jonah to go to Nineveh, he said, "No way!"

Jonah loved the Lord. The Ninevites? Not so much! They were wicked, too far gone in Jonah's mind. *They'll never listen if I tell them to turn from their sins and turn to God. Why go?* Jonah must have thought. *And how could God love* them *and forgive* them?

So instead of listening to God, Jonah ran away from God. He boarded a boat to Tarshish and sailed in the opposite direction. But the Lord was about to show Jonah how serious His love really is for all people—even for people in the big city of Nineveh.

Jonah's boat rocked back and forth. The waves got higher and hit the boat harder—until finally Jonah cried out, "Throw me overboard. This is my fault!" Sure enough, the storm stopped when he went over. And when Jonah cried out to God, the Lord saved him. He sent a large fish that swallowed Jonah, protecting him for three days and three nights before spitting him out onto dry land.

This time when God said, "Go!" Jonah listened. And much to his surprise, the people of Nineveh listened too. Jonah learned that no one is too far gone for God. He has compassion for all people, and so should we!

LET'S DISCUSS TOGETHER

- *Why didn't Jonah want to go to Nineveh?*
- *What did Jonah learn about God's heart?*
- *What are one or two things you can do to love someone far from God?*

LET'S PRAY TOGETHER

Lord, You are full of compassion and mercy. You don't just love some people, You love all people. Help us have Your heart. Teach us to love others the same way You love us. In Jesus' name, amen.

● ● ● ● ● ● ●

For Further Study: Jonah 1-4

44

TRUSTING GOD IN TRIALS

• • • • • • • • •

The Lord gave and the Lord has taken away; may the name of the Lord be praised.

JOB 1:21

Sometimes life can really hurt, can't it? We can go through hard or sad times. When life gets tough, we can wonder what God is doing. Or we might ask ourselves, *Why me?* Job's life is a good example of how to trust God in the middle of trials.

Job was a blessed man. He had a big family. He was very wealthy. His health was good. Job loved God. He was righteous. Blameless. Everything seemed to be going right for Job. But what would Job do when everything started to go wrong?

God allowed Satan to test Job's faith—to see if Job loved Him even when things were not going well.

Things started to go really wrong for Job! He lost some of his family whom he loved so much. His house burned down. A large fire burned up a lot of his possessions. Even his health began to fail. Just about everything that could go wrong did go wrong.

So wrong that even Job's wife told him he should give up on God. "Curse God and die!" she shouted. His friends were not much help either.

They wondered if maybe God was punishing Job for something he did wrong.

Job would not give up on God though. Of course he was sad and cried out to God. But in the middle of it all, he kept trusting the Lord. And guess what? God blessed Job again. He gave him back everything he lost and even more!

The Lord reminded Job, just as He reminds us, that He is good. He is powerful. We might not always understand what He is doing, but God's plans are perfect. We can trust Him even in the trials.

KEY IDEA

God is in control. When we go through hard times, we need to remember that God is doing something. He has a plan and a purpose. We might not understand it, but we can trust it because we know God's heart is good.

LET'S DISCUSS TOGETHER

- *Why do people get mad at God?*
- *What helped Job trust God in his trials?*
- *What do we need to remember when we face hard times?*

LET'S PRAY TOGETHER

Father, we love You because of who You are and what You have done for us. Give us faith. Help us trust You and love You even when life is hard. In Jesus' name, amen.

• • • • • • •

For Further Study: Job 1–2

45

GOD IS HOLY

• • • • • • • • •

Holy, holy, holy is the LORD Almighty; the whole earth is full of his glory.

ISAIAH 6:3

The Israelites were at it again. They were supposed to be a light—showing all the nations around them what God is like. Instead, they had become just like all the nations around them. They had failed to be different, set apart—holy.

One day Isaiah, a prophet of God, saw something unusual. God gave him a vision. It was like a sneak peek into heaven, where God was seated on His throne. It scared Isaiah. Terrified him, actually. Winged creatures surrounded God in all His glory. Smoke swirled. The doorposts in the temple shook and rattled. The heavens thundered with praise and worship. Everyone was singing: "Holy, holy, holy is the LORD Almighty; the whole earth is full of his glory."

Isaiah knew he was nothing like God. He was unclean and sinful—the opposite of who God is! But God forgave him. And He told him he was to go warn the Israelites to turn back to God, to return to His love. If they didn't, they would be taken into exile—to live outside the land God had given them.

But it wasn't all bad news. There was good news too. A Savior was coming. In all of this turning back and forth to God, there would be a Savior who would come and turn their hearts back to God for good.

God is not indifferent to our sin. But like the Israelites, we could never be holy on our own.

We need a Savior: a Savior who will come and make us holy, washing us clean from our sins. Only Jesus can fully and finally take away our sins—which is exactly the hope God was offering us through Isaiah.

KEY IDEA

God is holy. To be holy is to be set apart or different from everyone else. This includes God being completely set apart from anything sinful or evil. To make sure we really understand this, the Bible repeats the word three times by saying God is holy, holy, holy!

LET'S DISCUSS TOGETHER

- *What does it mean to be holy?*
- *Why was Isaiah so scared?*
- *How does Jesus make us holy?*

LET'S PRAY TOGETHER

Lord God, there is no one like You. You are more powerful, wise, loving, and pure than anyone. Thank You for making us holy and forgiving us by our faith in Jesus. Help us live differently, set apart for You. In Jesus' name, amen.

● ● ● ● ● ● ●

For Further Study: Isaiah 6–9

46

A MORE POWERFUL KINGDOM IS COMING

• • • • • • • • •

In the time of those kings, the God of heaven will set up a kingdom that will never be destroyed, nor will it be left to another people. It will crush all those kingdoms and bring them to an end, but it will itself endure forever.

DANIEL 2:44

W hen was the last time you were really afraid? The Israelites were living in a scary place with a scary king ruling over them. King Nebuchadnezzar had taken many of them out of their land to Babylon.

One night King Nebuchadnezzar couldn't sleep. He tossed and turned. He had just had a dream he couldn't understand. He called in all his wise men, and they scratched their heads too, unable to figure it out. Exploding in anger, he ordered all of them to be killed unless someone could explain the meaning.

Once again God put one of His people in the right place at the right time. Daniel pleaded with God to reveal the mystery. And sure enough, He did. "You had a dream," Daniel said, "about a statue. Its head was gold, its chest and arms were silver, the middle was bronze. And the legs and feet were made of iron and clay."

That wasn't all! "In your dream," Daniel continued, "a rock crushed the statue and began to grow and grow into a big mountain. The rock is

God's kingdom. Your kingdom, and others after yours, will fall. Not God's. His kingdom will last forever!"

God was reminding His people, and Nebuchadnezzar, there is a more powerful kingdom coming. There is hope, no matter how scary things look. God is still King over all. And His kingdom will go on and on forever.

LET'S DISCUSS TOGETHER

- *What do you get scared about? Why?*
- *What do you think was most difficult or scary for the Israelites when they lived in a different land that worshipped different gods?*
- *Why is it comforting to know God is King?*

LET'S PRAY TOGETHER

Father, You are our great King. You are still in charge, ruling over all creation. You are more powerful and wise than any ruler on earth. We love You and trust You. We look forward to being with You someday in Your kingdom forever. In Jesus' name, amen.

• • • • • • •

For Further Study: Daniel 2

47

WE WILL NOT BOW DOWN!

• • • • • • • • •

If we are thrown into the blazing furnace, the God we serve is able to deliver us from it, and he will deliver us from Your Majesty's hand. But even if he does not, we want you to know, Your Majesty, that we will not serve your gods or worship the image of gold you have set up.

DANIEL 3:17-18

W hat would you do if it was against the law to live for God? Sometimes there is a cost or sacrifice for following the Lord. In Babylon, it almost cost three men their lives.

Nasty King Nebuchadnezzar forgot about God. He ignored his dream. Instead, he built a great big golden statue—nearly ninety feet high and nine feet wide. With pride, he announced to everyone:

As soon as you hear the sound of the horn, flute, zither, lyre, harp, pipe and all kinds of music, you must fall down and worship the image of gold. . . . Whoever does not fall down and worship will immediately be thrown into a blazing furnace. (Daniel 3:5–6)

Everyone listened . . . well, almost, everyone. Shadrach, Meshach, and Abednego refused to bow down. Even if God didn't rescue them, they were not backing down. And so in a fit of anger, King Nebuchadnezzar threw them into the flames.

KEY IDEA

God is our Helper. The God of the Bible is always with us, even when we don't see Him. He is our Defender, able to save us and protect us when we are in trouble.

But much to his surprise, when he stared into the flames, he saw four men, not three. A messenger of God was with them. Ordering them out, he couldn't believe they were completely safe.

Are you ever afraid of what people think of you? Don't be! It is always better to fear God more than people. While there might be a cost to living for God, what we gain by living for Him is far greater!

LET'S DISCUSS TOGETHER

- *When have you ever been afraid of others?*
- *Why were these men unafraid of the king?*
- *What are examples of "costs" when following Jesus?*

LET'S PRAY TOGETHER

Lord, You are our refuge and our Defender. Be with us and protect us. And give us the courage to live for You no matter what others may think or do. In Jesus' name, amen.

● ● ● ● ● ● ●

For Further Study: Daniel 3

48

PEOPLE ARE WATCHING!

· · · · · · · · ·

My God sent his angel, and he shut the mouths of the lions. They have not hurt me, because I was found innocent in his sight. Nor have I ever done any wrong before you, Your Majesty.

DANIEL 6:22

Who do you look up to? Why? Whether we know it or not, people are watching us. It might be a friend at school, a teammate, maybe a neighbor, or a family member. And people are not just watching us; people are being influenced by us.

Daniel was a man who loved God. And people noticed. In fact, when a different king in Babylon, Darius, came to power, he was so impressed with Daniel that he put him in charge. But this made the other leaders mad—so mad that they talked Darius into making a new law.

If anyone worshipped a different god, he or she would be thrown into the lions' den. Like Shadrach, Meshach, and Abednego, Daniel wasn't buying it. He had no fear—just faith. He didn't care what anyone did to him; he was going to worship the Lord alone!

But here's what happened. God was with Daniel. He shut the mouths of the lions. He came to his defense. And best of all, King Darius noticed! When he saw Daniel's faith and God's power, he wrote a letter to all the nations that said:

"I issue a decree that in every part of my kingdom people must fear and reverence the God of Daniel. For he is the living God and he endures forever; his kingdom will not be destroyed, his dominion will never end. He rescues and he saves." (Daniel 6:26–27)

A lot of people were able to hear about the one true God—all because of one faithful person, Daniel.

God just wants us to be faithful. Set apart for Him. He takes care of the rest! Who is watching you? What do they see?

LET'S DISCUSS TOGETHER

- *How has someone else influenced you?*
- *What was different about Daniel's faith?*
- *How can God use our example today to influence others?*

LET'S PRAY TOGETHER

Lord, You are our King. We want to serve You only. Remind us that people around us are watching how we live and love. Help our lives to point others to You. In Jesus' name, amen.

• • • • • •

For Further Study: Daniel 6

49

A QUEEN WHO WOULDN'T STAY SILENT

• • • • • • • • •

If you remain silent at this time, relief and deliverance for the Jews
will arise from another place, but you and your father's family
will perish. And who knows but that you have come to your royal
position for such a time as this?

ESTHER 4:14

It was no accident when Esther became the queen of Persia, the wife of King Xerxes. She was beautiful and smart. Most importantly, she loved God. She also happened to be an Israelite.

Esther didn't know why that was so important, but she would soon find out.

One of King Xerxes' rulers didn't like God's people. His name was Haman. He came up with a plan to have all the Israelites killed. Every single one. Wiped out. Completely destroyed. But there was one small problem: Esther's cousin, Mordecai, learned about Haman's evil plan.

"You've got to say something, Esther," Mordecai pleaded. "Who knows, this may be the very reason why *you* are the queen right *now*!"

Esther had a choice to make: she could speak up or stay quiet. Going to the king could be dangerous. *What will he do when he finds out I am an Israelite?* she wondered. But Esther did it anyway. She was convinced that God had put her in the palace for a purpose. And that purpose wasn't to stay quiet!

When King Xerxes found out about the plot to kill the Israelites, he was furious. Haman's plan backfired. And instead of God's people perishing, Haman was punished. God saved His people through one woman who refused to stay silent.

KEY IDEA

God has us where He wants us. God wants to use *you*, right where you are, to show and tell others what He is like.

Who are the people God has placed in your life? Just like Esther, God has placed each of us where we are for a reason. Don't stay quiet. Love and serve those around you. You never know why God has placed you right where *you* are!

LET'S DISCUSS TOGETHER

- *Why was it dangerous for Esther to speak up?*
- *What does it say about God that Esther became the queen when she did?*
- *Who are the people you think God has placed in your life for a reason?*

LET'S PRAY TOGETHER

Father, You have us where we are for a reason. Use our words, our attitudes, and our whole lives to lead others toward You. In Jesus' name, amen.

• • • • • •

For Further Study: Esther 1–10

50

THE GOD WHO RESTORES

• • • • • • • • •

They said to me, "Those who survived the exile and are back in the province are in great trouble and disgrace. The wall of Jerusalem is broken down, and its gates have been burned with fire."

NEHEMIAH 1:3

Jerusalem was a mess. The temple was in ruins, and so were the walls that surrounded their capital city.

One man, Nehemiah, wept when he heard that Jerusalem's walls were in such a bad state. He prayed. He confessed the sins that the Israelites had committed. And he even asked to lead some of God's people back to Jerusalem to rebuild the broken-down walls.

But before God would do a great work through Nehemiah, He would do a great work *in* Nehemiah. He softened his heart. Opened it up to what God wanted and what God was doing in the world.

This is where all of God's great works start: right inside each of us by giving us hearts of love and compassion—hearts that care for the things God cares about, hearts that are focused on others, and hearts that really want to trust and serve God.

God's people had been in exile, living outside of the promised land for years and years because their hearts had grown cold. But God promised that one day He would bring them home. He would rebuild their city, rebuild the temple, and most importantly, forgive His people, making them new again, once and for all! That day was coming soon.

Like Jerusalem's walls, no one is ever too broken down for God. No one is ever too far away for God to forgive. God loves to rebuild and renew lives. This is what God did for His people, and it's what He still does for us through our trust in Jesus.

LET'S DISCUSS TOGETHER

- *Why were God's people in exile?*
- *How did God change Nehemiah's heart?*
- *What areas of your life need to be "rebuilt" by God?*

LET'S PRAY TOGETHER

Lord, You are our Father and Friend. Thank You for Your love that never ends. It doesn't stop. Continue to change our hearts, making them new so we always please You. In Jesus' name, amen.

• • • • • •

For Further Study: Ezra 1; Jeremiah 29:10–14; Nehemiah 1

51

THE WAITING IS ALMOST OVER

• • • • • • • • •

Praise be to the Lord, the God of Israel, because he has come to his people and redeemed them.

LUKE 1:68

When was the last time you had to wait for something? How long did you have to wait? God's people knew a thing or two about waiting. They had been waiting a *long* time for God to send the Messiah, the Savior.

They knew God had made a promise to Adam and Eve that a child would come to destroy the works of Satan one day. And they knew from the promises the Lord had made to Abraham, Isaac, and Jacob that a child would one day bring salvation to all people, not just Israel. He would be from the tribe of Judah. A child from the house of David. A different kind of king with a kingdom that would go on and on forever!

Well, their waiting was almost over. But first God would send a messenger, John the Baptist, to prepare the way for Jesus.

John's parents weren't exactly young, which is why they couldn't believe their ears, or eyes, when an angel appeared to them and told them that they would have a child. John's father, Zechariah, was a priest working in the temple. John's mother, Elizabeth, had been without children. But both loved God and had been praying for this day for years.

And sure enough—God kept His word. Elizabeth would give birth to a son. And just as he was told, Zechariah named him John. As John grew up, he announced the coming of Jesus. The waiting was finally over!

What are you waiting for? Zechariah and Elizabeth never gave up on God when they were waiting. They trusted Him and remained obedient because they knew someday God would do what He said He was going to do!

KEY IDEA

God is faithful. It had been hundreds of years since God's people began to return to the promised land. It had been thousands of years since many of God's first promises about a Savior. But God is faithful, and we should remain faithful to Him even when we have to wait.

LET'S DISCUSS TOGETHER

- *When was a time you had to wait?*
- *What is an example of waiting the wrong way?*
- *How did John's parents wait the right way?*

LET'S PRAY TOGETHER

Father, You always do what You say You are going to do. When we have to wait, help us wait in faith. Teach us to be obedient, always serving You and never doubting You. In Jesus' name, amen.

● ● ● ● ● ●

For Further Study: Luke 1

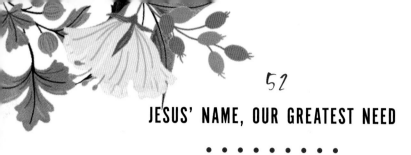

52

JESUS' NAME, OUR GREATEST NEED

• • • • • • • • •

"She will give birth to a son, and you are to give him the name
Jesus, because he will save his people from their sins." All this took
place to fulfill what the Lord had said through the prophet: "The
virgin will conceive and give birth to a son, and they will call him
Immanuel" (which means "God with us").

MATTHEW 1:21–23

Mary couldn't believe she was pregnant. After all, she and Joseph
were not even married yet. And that wasn't all. She was pregnant through the Holy Spirit. The baby boy inside of her was a gift from
God—God's own Son, Jesus.

Joseph was a righteous man. He was afraid of how it might look
for Mary to be pregnant before marriage, so he considered calling off
the wedding. But an angel appeared to him in a dream and explained
the miracle that was happening, the miracle that was growing inside of
Mary's womb—the miracle that would change the world forever.

The angel said, "Joseph son of David, do not be afraid to take Mary
home as your wife . . . because she will give birth to a son, and you are to
give him the name Jesus, because he will save his people from their sins"
(Matthew 1:20–21). He will also be called "Immanuel," which means
"God with us."

And so Joseph did as he was told. Soon after, Mary gave birth to Jesus and put him in a tiny little manger, in a tiny little stable, in a tiny little town called Bethlehem. But the birth of Jesus was no small event!

His name means "Savior," a reminder of our greatest need. We might think we need more money. Better friends. New shoes. But our greatest need is to be forgiven! And that is what Jesus was coming to do: to take away our sins once and for all.

KEY IDEA

Jesus is eternal. Jesus didn't begin to exist at His birth. He has always existed (John 1:1–4). He became like us at His birth, becoming human. Jesus "took on flesh," or became human, to show us what God is like in a way we could understand.

LET'S DISCUSS TOGETHER

- *Whose family was Joseph from, and why is that important?*
- *What did the angel say that Jesus would do?*
- *What is important about Jesus being called "Immanuel"?*

LET'S PRAY TOGETHER

Father, we praise You for loving us so much. Our greatest need is to know You and be forgiven by You. Thank You for giving us the gift of Your Son so we could be a part of Your family. In Jesus' name, amen.

● ● ● ● ● ● ●

For Further Study: Matthew 1:18–25; John 1:1–4

53

BOWING DOWN TO KING JESUS

• • • • • • • • •

After Jesus was born in Bethlehem in Judea, during the time of
King Herod, Magi from the east came to Jerusalem and asked,
"Where is the one who has been born king of the Jews? We saw his
star when it rose and have come to worship him."

MATTHEW 2:1-2

Have you ever seen something that no one else did? What was it,
and why did everyone else miss it? Shortly after Jesus was born,
some wise men saw something out of the ordinary in the sky. They knew
it was a sign, a special sign—one that they did not want to miss.

What did it mean exactly? They knew it was pointing to the arrival
of Jesus, King of the Jews. So they packed up their gear, loaded their
camels, and traveled to Jerusalem to see a different king, a lesser king,
named King Herod.

"We've come to worship the king of the Jews," they said. Herod was
not happy. He thought *he* was the king. But there is only one real King,
a humble King who had come to lead His people back to following God.

The wise men looked up and spotted the star again. Step by step
they followed it, growing more excited to meet the real King. When the
star finally stopped over a house, first they saw Mary, and then they saw
Jesus.

Joy exploded in their hearts. This King was different and they knew it, whether anyone else saw it or not! These wise men bowed down and worshipped Jesus with gifts. Their eyes saw the beauty, power, and worth of Jesus.

We might not bring gifts of gold, frankincense, or myrrh, but we can give Jesus the gift of our lives, loving and serving Him each day.

KEY IDEA

Jesus is our King. Jesus is not only our Savior, but He is also our King. We no longer live just for ourselves but, most importantly, for Him!

LET'S DISCUSS TOGETHER

- *What did the wise men see that no one else did?*
- *What does it mean to worship Jesus with our lives?*
- *What is one area of your life where Jesus needs to be in charge?*

LET'S PRAY TOGETHER

Jesus, loving You is more important than anything else. You are our Savior but also our King. Help us serve You and honor You in all we do. In Jesus' name, amen.

• • • • • •

For Further Study: Matthew 2:1–12; Micah 5:2

54

GROWING UP

• • • • • • • •

Jesus grew in wisdom and stature, and in favor with God and man.
LUKE 2:52

Mary and Joseph were crammed in the middle of the crowds, and so was Jesus. But at some point, when the Passover festival was over and His parents were heading home, Jesus wandered off. It took Joseph and Mary a day to figure out He was not with them.

Returning to Jerusalem, they spotted Him. He wasn't goofing off or hanging out with friends. He was in the temple—listening to and asking questions of the religious leaders. People were amazed with Jesus because He was only twelve.

But then His parents showed up. "Didn't you know your father and I were looking for you?" asked His mother. With respect, Jesus answered, "Didn't you know I had to be in *My* Father's house?" Jesus knew He was God's Son. He knew God the Father had sent Him as Savior and King. But He also knew His time had not yet come. So He obeyed His parents, following them all the way home this time.

We're not told a lot about Jesus' childhood. But we are told that He went home and grew in "wisdom and stature, and in favor with God and man." God the Father was preparing Him, getting Him ready for His work in the world.

God does the same with us. The ways He is growing us today is important for how God will use us in the future!

You might not know it yet. You might not be able to see it yet. But God is teaching you and preparing you for a work He wants to do through you. So keep growing. Keep learning. Keep loving God. He has big plans for you that you can't see right now.

KEY IDEA

Jesus knew He was the Son of God. From an early age, Jesus knew that He was God's Son sent to accomplish the work of God the Father.

LET'S DISCUSS TOGETHER

- *In what ways do you think Jesus grew?*
- *Why is it important to keep growing now so we can be used by God later?*
- *What is one way you can continue to grow in your relationship with God?*

LET'S PRAY TOGETHER

Father, continue to teach us. Help us grow in our knowledge of You and our love for You. We want You to work through us now and as we grow older. In Jesus' name, amen.

• • • • • •

For Further Study: Luke 2:41-52

55

THE BAPTISM OF JESUS

• • • • • • • • •

A voice from heaven said, "This is my Son, whom I love; with him I am well pleased."

MATTHEW 3:17

Has anyone ever given you a nickname? What is it, and why did they give it to you? As Zechariah and Elizabeth's son, John, grew up, he too was given a nickname. He was known as John the Baptist because people from all over came to him to say they were sorry for their sins and be baptized by him in the Jordan River.

John's clothing was made of camel's hair. A belt of leather was wrapped around his waist. Locusts and wild honey were his favorite foods. Instead of hanging out in the temple, John wandered around the desert of Judea, preaching about how God's Son, Jesus, was coming soon—coming to lead people back to friendship with God.

You can imagine why John was so surprised when Jesus showed up to be baptized by him! "I need to be baptized by *You*!" John said. "No," Jesus said. "This is the way it is supposed to be." So instead of Jesus baptizing John, John baptized Jesus.

The sky tore open like a curtain, and John saw the Holy Spirit coming down on Jesus like a dove. And then he heard a voice. Not just any voice. He heard the warm and powerful voice of God the Father say, "This is My Son. I love Him and I am pleased with Him!"

Right there in the middle of the water, with all the sinners—there was Jesus. Why? Because Jesus came to save sinners. And He was showing them that He was with them and for them, not against them. He was going to wash away their sins. But it wouldn't be with water; it would be with His blood on the cross one day.

KEY IDEA

God the Father loves us. Just as God the Father speaks words of love over Jesus, He does the same over us. He is pleased with us not because we are perfect but because we have trusted in His perfect Son. We are like sons and daughters of God!

LET'S DISCUSS TOGETHER

- *Why did John want Jesus to baptize him?*
- *Why was it important for God the Father to speak over Jesus?*
- *What does Jesus' baptism say about His love?*

LET'S PRAY TOGETHER

Father, thank You for making us a part of Your family. We know that You love us and sent Jesus to save us. Help us never doubt Your love for us. In Jesus' name, amen.

• • • • • •

For Further Study: Matthew 3

121

56

BATTLE IN THE DESERT

• • • • • • • • •

The reason the Son of God appeared was to destroy the devil's work.

1 JOHN 3:8

M ountains were stretched out in every direction. It was hot. Rocks and sand covered everything. Jesus had just been baptized, and now He was alone in the desert.

He wasn't lost. The Holy Spirit had led Him into the desert—for a battle. And He wasn't alone for long. The Devil came to tempt Him, just as he had been tempting everyone from the beginning. But this battle would end differently.

Three times the Devil came to Jesus and said, "If You are the Son of God . . ."

"Tell these stones to become bread."

"Throw Yourself down from the top of the temple."

"Bow down and worship me."

But three times Jesus answered Satan's tricks with the truth of God's Word.

The Devil is an expert in trapping people in sin, stealing the life and joy that God wants to give. But Jesus wouldn't fall for it. In the garden, Adam and Eve sinned. In the desert, Jesus won.

Jesus came to defeat the Devil, and this was just was the beginning. He came to undo the sadness caused by sin, stop the lies, and push back the darkness. We may fight an Enemy, but he is an Enemy on the run. An Enemy who has lost his power.

When we become Christians, God gives us His Spirit so we can say no to sin. And because Jesus has won the battle, with His help, we can win ours as well!

LET'S DISCUSS TOGETHER

- *What was the Devil trying to get Jesus to do?*
- *How did Jesus stand strong against temptation?*
- *How do we help undo the works of the Devil?*

LET'S PRAY TOGETHER

Lord, You are the One who strengthens us and protects us. Give us power though Your Spirit to live for You each day. Give us wisdom to see temptation and grace to turn to You. In Jesus' name, amen.

• • • • • •

For Further Study: Matthew 4:1–11; Luke 4:1–13

57

JESUS' FIRST FOLLOWERS

• • • • • • • • •

"Come, follow me," Jesus said, "and I will send you out to fish for people." At once they left their nets and followed him.

MATTHEW 4:19-20

Is there someone you look up to? What is it about that person that makes you want to be like him or her? Everyone is following someone. It might be a friend, a family member, or maybe even someone on TV. All of us are followers—what matters most is *who* we are following!

After Jesus' forty days and forty nights in the desert, He began to look for others to join Him in God's work in the world. He was looking for followers, or disciples. A disciple is like a student, a really good student. Not just someone who wants to have all the right answers, but a student who wants to learn from Jesus and learn to be like Jesus. Disciples want to love God with all of their heart, soul, strength, and mind.

As Jesus was walking along the Sea of Galilee, He saw two brothers—Peter and Andrew. "Come follow Me," He said. They dropped their nets and followed Jesus. Two more brothers, James and John, became disciples of Jesus too, leaving behind their boat, fishing nets, and father!

Jesus first chose twelve disciples. Some of them left family. Others their jobs and their friends. The invitation to be a part of what God was doing in the world was too good to pass up, no matter what they had to leave behind. They wanted to be "fishers of men," telling others about God's amazing love and forgiveness.

So who are you following? Jesus is still looking for disciples who want to learn from Him and learn to be like Him, people who want to live for others and not just themselves.

KEY IDEA

Jesus invites imperfect people to follow Him. Jesus didn't choose perfect people. He invites ordinary and everyday people like us. But as we learn from Him, He changes us and makes us more and more like Him!

LET'S DISCUSS TOGETHER

- *What does it mean to be a student of Jesus?*
- *How can you learn from Him?*
- *How do you need to be more like Him?*

LET'S PRAY TOGETHER

Lord, thank You for asking us to follow You, trust in You, and learn from You. Continue to change us and make us more like You. In Jesus' name, amen.

● ● ● ● ● ●
For Further Study: Matthew 4:18–22; Luke 5:1–11

125

58

LET YOUR LIGHT SHINE!

• • • • • • • • •

"Let your light shine before others, that they may see your good
deeds and glorify your Father in heaven."

MATTHEW 5:16

Shortly after Jesus chose His first disciples, He went up on a mountain with them and sat down. A large crowd gathered around Him.
And because Jesus' mission in the world is so important, He began to
teach them how to live with God in charge of their lives.

You are blessed or truly happy when you are humble or poor in spirit.
When you mourn, God will comfort you.
Don't be pushy, but be meek and gentle with others.
If you hunger and thirst to do what is right, God will satisfy you.
Blessed are you when you show mercy and make peace.
If people make fun of you or mistreat you, rejoice because great is
your reward in heaven.

And then Jesus reminded His disciples of how dark the world can be.
People are hurting. Many feel lost or confused. They don't know about
God's love and forgiveness. So Jesus said to His disciples:

"You are the light of the world. A city set on a hill cannot be hidden.
Nor do people light a lamp and put it under a basket, but on a stand,

and it gives light to everyone in the house. In the same way, let your light shine before others, that they may see your good deeds and glorify your Father in heaven." (Matthew 5:14–16)

What do others see in you? Is there anything different about how you live, talk, and treat others? Jesus is the Light of the World, and because He lives in us, He is shining His light through us!

KEY IDEA

Jesus is the Light of the World. We don't have to guess what God is like. Jesus shows us who He is and how we can know Him. Jesus is shining His light through us, helping others see and know God too.

LET'S DISCUSS TOGETHER

- *Why is it important for us to live differently?*
- *What does Jesus say can happen when we live differently?*
- *What is one way you can be a light to someone?*

LET'S PRAY TOGETHER

Heavenly Father, help us let You be in charge of our lives. Teach us to live differently so others see the light of Jesus in us. Where there is darkness, let Your love and life shine to bring joy and hope. In Jesus' name, amen.

● ● ● ● ● ●

For Further Study: Matthew 5:1–16

59

LOVE IS STRONGER

• • • • • • • • •

"But I tell you, love your enemies and pray for those who persecute you."

MATTHEW 5:44

Do you know someone who is hard to love? Maybe it's someone who has a different personality or a friend who did something or said something that was hurtful to you. How do you treat this person?

Sometimes we like to get even. If people hurt us, we might want to hurt them back. Or we can be tempted to just end a friendship. To stay away from someone or say things behind someone's back. But Jesus teaches us a different way—a better way.

Jesus taught that love is powerful. Love can melt someone's hard heart. It can change someone's attitude. Love can overcome evil. It's easy to love those who love us but far more powerful and beautiful to love the unlovable.

We can pray for someone who has hurt us. We can do good to someone even if he or she has wronged us. We can respond with kind words. We can bless someone by loving him or her when the person doesn't deserve it.

This kind of love is not only powerful; it's possible! How? Because this is exactly how God has loved us. Jesus says to "be merciful, just as your Father is merciful" (Luke 6:36). And this love of God lives in us.

Following Jesus is about trusting what He says. It's about believing God's way of living is far better than our way of living!

How will you love someone who is hard to love? Resist the temptation to get back at others. Instead, pray for them. Pray for your own heart. Pray that Jesus would help you love others the way He has loved you.

KEY IDEA

Treat others the way you want to be treated (Luke 6:31). How do you want to be treated by someone else? How do you like someone to talk to you? Jesus told us the best way to treat others, including our enemies, is the way we want to be treated!

LET'S DISCUSS TOGETHER

- *What are ways that people try to get even?*
- *How can love change someone's heart?*
- *In what ways has God treated us better than we deserve?*

LET'S PRAY TOGETHER

Lord, teach us to love and forgive those who mistreat us. Fill us with Your Holy Spirit so we can do good, be prayerful, and bless others. In Jesus' name, amen.

● ● ● ● ● ● ●

For Further Study: Matthew 5:43–48; Luke 6:27–36

60

LEARNING TO PRAY

· · · · · · · · ·

"When you pray, go into your room, close the door and pray to
your Father, who is unseen."

MATTHEW 6:6

W here do you go when you need help? At some point in our lives,
we realize there are some things we just can't fix on our own. We
need someone bigger, stronger, and wiser to help us.

That someone is God our Father. Jesus reminds us that we are not
alone in the world. We were created by a Father who loves us, watches
over us, never leaves us, and is always there for us. And He is also a God
who wants to have a relationship with us.

Prayer is one important way to grow our relationship with God. He
knows we can be tempted to forget Him. We depend on our own strength
or knowledge. So when Jesus' first disciples were trying to understand
how to talk to God in prayer, He told them to pray like this:

Our Father in heaven, hallowed be your name,
your kingdom come, your will be done, on earth as it is in heaven.
Give us today our daily bread.
And forgive us our debts, as we also have forgiven our debtors.
And lead us not into temptation, but deliver us from the evil one.
(Matthew 6:9–13)

One of the ways God loves us is by listening to us. He wants us to take our problems to Him: to run to Him with our fears, to ask for guidance, to seek His power, and to trust His plans. When we pray, we can be sure God hears us, cares about us, and is working in us.

KEY IDEA

God loves us by listening to us. We can be sure God hears us when we pray to Him. He cares about what is going on in our lives and is active in ways we don't always see.

LET'S DISCUSS TOGETHER

- *Why do you think some people don't pray?*
- *How does prayer change us?*
- *What is one thing our family can be praying about?*

LET'S PRAY TOGETHER

Father, thank You that we can come to You with our needs and worries. You know us and love us. Continue to change our hearts to be more like Yours. Help us grow closer to You, and teach us to trust You, for You are stronger and wiser than we are. In Jesus' name, amen.

• • • • • • •

For Further Study: Matthew 6:5-15; Luke 11:1-4

61

LOVING PEOPLE MORE THAN POSSESSIONS

• • • • • • • • •

"Where your treasure is, there your heart will be also."
MATTHEW 6:21

What is most important to you? What makes you the happiest? Is it a favorite sport you play, a show you watch, clothes you own, or a possession you have? While Jesus was still teaching His disciples on the mountain, He taught them a very important lesson about what should be their greatest treasure.

Jesus knew we would be tempted to make our possessions (what we own) more important than people, which is why He told His disciples to be careful of just storing up treasure here on earth. He reminded them that stuff gets old, breaks, cracks, dents, and gets dirty. And most important of all, we can't take our stuff to heaven with us.

But guess what we can take to heaven? What we do for God and for other people! This is why Jesus taught us to be generous and rich in good deeds. There is nothing wrong with having possessions or money. What God wants is for us to bless and serve others with what He has given us, instead of just using it for ourselves. This is how we "store up . . . treasures in heaven" (Matthew 6:20).

"Where your treasure is," Jesus said, "your heart will be also." Our lives will follow what we love. If we love video games, then we'll spend lots of time and energy and money playing games. If we love clothes, we'll spend lots of time and energy and money trying to look a certain way or always be in fashion. But loving God and people is the only thing that can truly make us happy!

So what will you treasure most? Will you treasure loving God and people? Or will you treasure your possessions? Our stuff is temporary treasure. Loving God and loving others is a treasure that lasts forever!

LET'S DISCUSS TOGETHER

- *How can people love possessions too much?*
- *How can someone be rich in good deeds?*
- *What is one way you can use what you have to bless someone else?*

LET'S PRAY TOGETHER

Lord, You are our greatest treasure. Nothing is more important to us than knowing You, loving You, and serving You. Continue to teach us to love people more than possessions. In Jesus' name, amen.

● ● ● ● ● ● ●

For Further Study: Matthew 6:19–24

62

WORRY LESS, TRUST MORE

. . . .

"I tell you, do not worry about your life, what you will eat or drink; or about your body, what you will wear. Is not life more than food, and the body more than clothes?"

MATTHEW 6:25

Everybody worries about something. It could be grades. Your friends. The future. What is it for you?

Jesus and His disciples were living during pretty hard times. Many of Abraham's descendants, the Jewish people, did not have a lot of money. The Romans were ruling over the land God had given the Israelites. And it was often dangerous to follow Jesus. There was a lot to worry about!

So when Jesus was teaching His disciples how to live for God, He told them to look around. Look around at what exactly? Well, for starters, He told them to look at the birds.

The birds don't look very stressed out, do they? They don't store up lots of food. See how your heavenly Father takes care of them? Don't worry about what you will eat. *You* are even more valuable than the birds of the air!

And look at the flowers. See how they are clothed? Don't worry about what you will wear. Life is more important that what you wear. Just like your heavenly Father takes care of the flowers, He will also take care of *you*.

There are many things in our lives that are out of our control. But God is in charge. And not only is He in charge, He cares for His children. Jesus doesn't want us to walk through life fearful and anxious. He wants to give us His life and joy and peace. And the only way we can experience that is by trusting our heavenly Father more and worrying less!

LET'S DISCUSS TOGETHER

- *What is one thing you worry about?*
- *How can trusting God help us worry less?*
- *What is one way to trust God more?*

LET'S PRAY TOGETHER

Heavenly Father, thank You for the reminder that You always take care of us. You have promised to take care of all our needs. Help us worry less and trust You more. In Jesus' name, amen.

● ● ● ● ● ● ●

For Further Study: Matthew 6:25–34; Luke 12:22–34

63

TWO BUILDERS

· · · · · · · · ·

"Everyone who hears these words of mine and puts them into
practice is like a wise man who built his house on the rock."

MATTHEW 7:24

Jesus taught His disciples many things. He was a masterful teacher, wanting His followers to experience the good life of knowing, loving, and serving God. But Jesus wants more than just to pass on information; Jesus wants transformation.

What does that look like? It looks like not only hearing Jesus' teachings but practicing them! To be sure His disciples understood clearly, He told them a story about two builders. One was a wise builder, and the other one was a foolish builder.

Jesus said the wise builder went out to build a house. This builder dug down into the earth. Then he dug a little deeper, until he hit rock. That's where he built his house—on the unmovable, strong, and sturdy foundation of rock. When a flood came, guess what happened to that house? It stood strong!

And then there was a foolish builder. This builder went out to build a house too. But instead of choosing a rock, he found some sandy soil. *Good enough*, he thought. With no foundation, he built his house. When the flood came, guess what happened to that house? It came crashing down!

Jesus taught that when we build our life on what He has said and promised, we are like the wise builder. Jesus' words are like a rock-solid foundation. When trouble comes, we will be unmoved.

So how will you build? Whose words will you listen to? Don't just hear God's Word; put it into practice!

KEY IDEA

True wisdom is not just knowing God's Word; it is obeying God's Word. God saves us to live with Him and for Him. He wants us to be not only hearers of His Word but doers of His Word!

LET'S DISCUSS TOGETHER

- *Why is just knowing information about God not enough?*
- *Why did Jesus say we need to hear and obey?*
- *What is one way you can build your life on "the rock"?*

LET'S PRAY TOGETHER

Dear Lord, we want to be like the wise builder who built his house on the rock. We don't want to just hear Your words; we want to put them into practice. In Jesus' name, amen.

• • • • • •

For Further Study: Matthew 7:24–29; Luke 6:46–49

64

THE GOD OF COMPASSION

• • • • • • • • •

Jesus reached out his hand and touched the man. "I am willing," he
said. "Be clean!" Immediately he was cleansed of his leprosy.

MATTHEW 8:3

Unclean, unclean," the man yelled as he walked toward a crowd of
people. He was warning them to stay away. He was sick and had to
let everyone else know so they wouldn't accidently touch him, becoming
unclean themselves.

He barely looked anyone in the eyes. He was forced to live outside the
city. Alone. Away from friends and family. Why? Because he had leprosy,
a terrible and often painful skin disease. He knew no one wanted him
around. That is, until he met Jesus.

As Jesus was coming down from the mountainside, the leper saw
Him. The sick man was scared that Jesus would turn him away too. That
He would reject him and send him back outside the city. Alone.

"If you are willing—if you want to," he said to Jesus, "I know you can
make me clean." The seconds he waited for Jesus' response must have felt
like hours. What would Jesus say? What would He do?

Much to the man's surprise, and with everyone watching, Jesus
did more than speak to him. He reached out His hand and touched
him. Instead of Jesus becoming unclean, the leper became clean. Full

of compassion, Jesus said, "I am willing. I care about you and want you to be healed."

Showing His power and proof that He really was God, Jesus cleansed the leper. But He also showed how much He cares.

Do you ever feel scared? Ever feel alone? Are you hurting? Don't forget that we serve a powerful God who is full of compassion for you!

LET'S DISCUSS TOGETHER

- *Who do you go to when you are hurting?*
- *Why is it important to remember that God is powerful and compassionate?*
- *How can you show compassion to others?*

LET'S PRAY TOGETHER

Heavenly Father, You are full of compassion toward us. You care about our struggles and pain. Comfort us when we are hurting. Help us remember You are with us and for us. In Jesus' name, amen.

● ● ● ● ● ● ●

For Further Study: Matthew 8:1–4; Mark 1:40–45; Luke 5:12–16

65

A POWERFUL FAITH

• • • • • • • • •

When Jesus heard this, he was amazed and said to those following him, "Truly I tell you, I have not found anyone in Israel with such great faith."

MATTHEW 8:10

J esus brought love, forgiveness, and hope for everyone. Not just some. Not just the Israelites. Everyone. He was, and is, the Savior of the whole world! That's what a Roman soldier found out when one of his servants was so sick that he became paralyzed.

Roman soldiers weren't exactly heroes in the eyes of the Jewish people. After all, they were living in their land—the land God had given Israel. And the Romans had a strong and powerful military, which made everyone feel a little uneasy with them around.

So when a Roman soldier asked Jesus to heal his servant, this made Jesus' response all the more amazing! The man said to Jesus, "I am not even worthy for you to come to my house. Just say the word and I know he will be healed."

Just as Jesus was willing to heal the leper, He was willing to heal the Roman soldier's servant. And not only that, Jesus was amazed at the man's faith. It was unlike anything Jesus had seen. This Roman soldier didn't doubt. He believed. He knew who Jesus was and what kind of power He really had. Jesus said to the soldier, "'Go! Let it be done just as you believed it would.' And his servant was healed at that moment" (Matthew 8:13).

The story of the Roman soldier reminds us what kind of faith God wants: a simple trust that God can do anything, even what seems impossible. But it's also a reminder that there is a place for everyone in God's kingdom. He is the Savior of the whole world!

KEY IDEA

Jesus wants our faith. Jesus doesn't always heal every disease or sickness. And He doesn't always give us what we want. But He wants us to have faith in His power and purposes. He is the same today and can still work miracles among His people.

LET'S DISCUSS TOGETHER

- *Why did the soldier feel unworthy?*
- *What kind of faith does God want?*
- *How does this story change the way you see other people?*

LET'S PRAY TOGETHER

Jesus, You are the Savior of the whole world. Thank You for Your power. Nothing is too hard for You. We trust You and believe You are the same yesterday, today, and tomorrow. In Jesus' name, amen.

● ● ● ● ● ●

For Further Study: Matthew 8:5–13; Luke 7:1–10

141

66

JESUS CALMS THE STORM

• • • • • • • • •

The men were amazed and asked, "What kind of man is this? Even
the winds and the waves obey him!"

MATTHEW 8:27

W hen was the last time you were really scared? What helped your
fear go away? Jesus' disciples found themselves in a pretty scary
situation one day. But it was also the kind of situation in which they
would learn one of their most valuable lessons about trusting God.

Everything was going great. Jesus was teaching them by the lake. It
was safe. No wind. No waves. Not much to worry about. And then Jesus
changed His location to teach them a new lesson.

Jesus got into a boat and told them to follow. "We're going to the
other side," He said. Not long after getting in the boat, Jesus fell asleep.
That's when the problems started. Instead of being safe on shore, they
were now in the middle of the lake.

The wind picked up, swirling around the boat. The waves crashed.
And then they crashed harder, rocking the boat back and forth. The
storm became so severe that the disciples thought they were going to die.
They woke Jesus, saying, "Master, Master, we're going to drown!" (Luke
8:24).

But Jesus stared the storm in the face, and He commanded the wind and waves to *stop*! And all went quiet. Just as quickly as the storm started, it ended. All was peaceful, quiet, and calm. The disciples were relieved but also scared.

"Who is this?" they wondered. "Even the wind and the waves listen to Him!"

Jesus asked His disciples a question. It's a question He still asks us today. "Where is your faith?" (v. 25). Jesus wants our trust when all is calm but also in the middle of the storm!

KEY IDEA

Jesus is fully God and fully human. The Bible teaches that Jesus had a human nature just like us—He got tired, He was thirsty, He had a body, He needed to eat, and things like that. But unlike us, He was fully God. And His miracles proved it! Just like with God, all creation listened and obeyed His words.

LET'S DISCUSS TOGETHER

- *Why did Jesus take the disciples onto the lake?*
- *What did they learn about Jesus in the storm?*
- *What "storm" do you want Jesus to calm?*

LET'S PRAY TOGETHER

Jesus, there is no one like You. You have power over all things. Even the wind and waves obey Your word. You have the strength to calm every storm, so help us trust You when we are afraid. In Jesus' name, amen.

● ● ● ● ● ●

For Further Study: Matthew 8:23–27; Mark 4:35–41; Luke 8:22–25

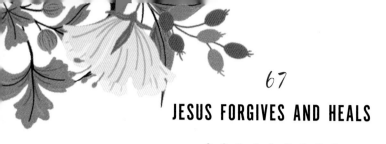

67

JESUS FORGIVES AND HEALS

• • • • • • • • •

When Jesus saw their faith, he said to the man, "Take heart, son; your sins are forgiven."

MATTHEW 9:2

Not long after Jesus arrived back on shore, He entered a nearby home. A crowed swarmed around the house so that no one else could get in and see Him. But that didn't stop several men who wanted to get their friend to Jesus! Their friend was sick, and he couldn't walk.

"When they could not find a way to do this because of the crowd, they went up on the roof and lowered him on his mat through the tiles into the middle of the crowd, right in front of Jesus" (Luke 5:19).

Jesus was not upset. He wasn't bothered with the crowd or the men. He was full of joy when He saw them because of their faith. These men had heard about Jesus and knew He had the power to help their friend walk again.

But Jesus did something they weren't expecting. Instead of telling the paralyzed man to get up and walk, Jesus said, "Take heart, son; your sins are forgiven" (Matthew 9:2).

Some of the religious leaders who heard Jesus were furious. "Only God can forgive sins!" they shouted. Jesus was once again proving that He was more than a prophet, teacher, or miracle worker.

Jesus didn't stop there. He forgave the man of his sins. But He also said, "Get up, take your mat and go home" (v. 6).

The man who was brought to Jesus thought his greatest need was to walk again. But really his greatest need was to be forgiven of his sins. When the crowds saw what Jesus did for the paralyzed man, they praised God, giving thanks for Jesus' miracle. But most importantly, they praised God for His power to forgive.

KEY IDEA

Our greatest need is to be forgiven. Jesus performed many miracles. He gave sight to the blind. Helped people speak again. Healed lepers. Raised the dead. And as we just saw, He made the lame walk. But the greatest miracle is forgiving us of our sins. Our greatest need is to be in a relationship with God!

LET'S DISCUSS TOGETHER

- *Why was Jesus pleased with the friends' faith?*
- *Has God ever given you what you needed instead of what you wanted?*
- *What is one way you can "carry" your friends to Jesus?*

LET'S PRAY TOGETHER

Heavenly Father, thank You for sending Jesus to be our Savior. We can bring all our needs to You, knowing You care for us. We praise You for meeting our greatest need—our need to be forgiven. In Jesus' name, amen.

• • • • • • •

For Further Study: Matthew 9:1–8; Mark 2:1–12; Luke 5:17–26

68

FRIEND OF SINNERS

• • • • • • • • •

"I have not come to call the righteous, but sinners."
MATTHEW 9:13

Do you have a friend who isn't a Christian? How about someone you know who you think would never follow Jesus?

Matthew was about the last guy you would expect to follow Jesus. He was a tax collector, which meant he collected money for the Romans. The Jewish people did not like tax collectors—they considered them sinners! But this isn't how Jesus saw Matthew.

One day Matthew was sitting at his tax collection booth, taking money and enjoying every minute of it. But his life was about to change for the better. Jesus walked up to him and with love in His eyes said, "Come follow Me."

Matthew didn't waste any time. He left his table. Said goodbye to his job. And most of all, he turned his back on his past for a better future with Jesus. He had just heard the best news there is: that God was for him and not against him.

The religious leaders scratched their heads. They were confused. Mad. They asked Jesus' disciples, "How could Jesus be a friend of such sinners? Doesn't He know what kind of man Matthew is?"

On hearing this, Jesus said, "It is not the healthy who need a doctor, but the sick" (Matthew 9:12).

God's heart is for people who are far from Him—people just like Matthew. There is no one who is too far gone. No matter what someone has done, where they have been, or who they used to be, God's love can change them. No matter what our past is, Jesus has a better future for us!

KEY IDEA

Jesus offers us a better future. Jesus offers us real life full of purpose, love, joy, peace, and hope. No matter what someone has done, he or she is never beyond God's love. What God offers us is so much better than living for ourselves!

LET'S DISCUSS TOGETHER

- *Why was Matthew an unlikely follower of Jesus?*
- *Why were the religious leaders upset?*
- *How can you reach out to a friend who is not following Jesus?*

LET'S PRAY TOGETHER

Heavenly Father, we are so grateful You loved us enough to send Jesus to die on the cross for us. You want everyone to know about Your love. Help us share Your love with our friends who don't know You yet. In Jesus' name, amen.

• • • • • •

For Further Study: Matthew 9:9-13; Mark 2:13-17; Luke 5:27-31

69

FOUR TYPES OF SOIL

• • • • • • • • •

"The seed falling on good soil refers to someone who hears the word and understands it. This is the one who produces a crop, yielding a hundred, sixty or thirty times what was sown."

MATTHEW 13:23

Jesus was a master at telling stories. Those kinds of stories make you think and ask yourself questions about how you are really living. The Bible refers to these stories as parables.

One day Jesus told a parable about a farmer who went out and threw seed on the ground. The seed fell on four very different kinds of soil. In Jesus' story, the seed was really God's Word, and the kinds of soil were four different types of hearts.

First the seed fell on hard ground like cement. Jesus said this is the heart that hears God's truth but doesn't believe it or accept it.

Then some of the farmer's seed fell on a rocky path. The seed began to grow but quickly died because it had no roots. Jesus said this kind of soil is like someone who turns away from God when trials or hard times come.

And then there was seed that fell among thorns. It grew but got choked out. This kind of heart, Jesus said, is the heart that is distracted. It's like a person who is too busy doing other things to follow God.

Finally, there was the good soil. It welcomed the seed. It allowed it to grow. This soil produced lots of fruit. Jesus was showing us that if we are going to partner with God in the world, we need to have this kind of heart—a heart that believes and obeys God's Word.

LET'S DISCUSS TOGETHER

- *How would you describe someone with a hard heart?*
- *How can we get distracted from following Jesus?*
- *Like a tree planted in good soil, how can we grow deep "roots" that grow our faith?*

LET'S PRAY TOGETHER

Heavenly Father, give us good hearts. Change us from the inside out. Give us hearts that hear, believe, and obey Your Word. We love You because You first loved us. In Jesus' name, amen.

• • • • • • •

For Further Study: Matthew 13:1–23; Mark 4:1–20; Luke 8:1–15

70

OUR GREATEST TREASURE

• • • • • • • • •

"The kingdom of heaven is like treasure hidden in a field. When a man found it, he hid it again, and then in his joy went and sold all he had and bought that field."

MATTHEW 13:44

W hen was the last time you found something? Maybe it was a toy you forgot you had or money on the street. What did you do? Jesus told another parable about a man who found something he was not expecting. And when he found it, it changed everything for him!

"There was a man," Jesus said, "who took a treasure and buried it in a field." We're not told what the treasure was, how much it was worth, or where the man put it. All we know is that it was very valuable.

One day another man was in the same field. He was probably working the field, maybe as a farmer. Suddenly, as he thrust his shovel into the earth, he heard a different noise. *Clunk. Clunk. Ding.* And then the sun hit a pile of gold, spraying bright light in every direction. He had hit treasure.

When he realized what he had found, he realized everything he had was not that important. It wasn't that valuable—not compared to the treasure he had just found. What did this man do next? He went and sold everything he owned so he could buy the field. The field was now his, and so was the treasure.

Finding Jesus is like finding the greatest treasure. Our greatest treasure is a Person! Nothing compares to knowing and loving Jesus. What He has done for us and will do for us one day is the most valuable thing we have. When we treasure Jesus more, we will treasure everything else less!

LET'S DISCUSS TOGETHER

- *What do you treasure?*
- *What does it look like to treasure Jesus more than everything else we have?*
- *What is one way we can show that Jesus is our greatest treasure?*

LET'S PRAY TOGETHER

Dear Lord, nothing compares to You. You are our greatest treasure—more important than anything else we have. Help us live for You and please You in all we do. In Jesus' name, amen.

● ● ● ● ● ● ●

For Further Study:
Matthew 13:44–46

71

THE GOOD SAMARITAN

• • • • • • • • •

"'Love the Lord your God with all your heart and with all your soul and with all your strength and with all your mind'; and, 'Love your neighbor as yourself.'"

LUKE 10:27

When was the last time you saw someone in need? How did you treat that person? One day several religious leaders tried to trick Jesus with a question. He had just told them that the most important commandment was to love God and love your neighbor. "Who is our neighbor?" they asked.

Once again, Jesus told a story:

"A man was traveling from Jerusalem to Jericho," Jesus said, "when he was robbed. They stripped him of everything. All his money, possessions, and even his clothes."

First, a priest, on his way home from the temple, saw the man. Seeing that he was badly hurt, the priest looked away. He stepped over him and passed by, leaving the man alone.

Then another religious man, a Levite, walked by. Surely he would stop! But he didn't either. Just like the priest, he passed by on the other side of the road.

The Jewish people did not like the Samaritans. So you can imagine how upset the religious leaders must have been when they heard it was a third traveler, a Samaritan, who stopped and helped. He put bandages on the man and even took him to an inn to take care of him.

"Which of these three do you think was a neighbor to the man who fell into the hands of robbers?" Jesus asked. The expert in the law replied, "The one who had mercy on him."

Jesus told him, "Go and do likewise" (Luke 10:36–37).

Jesus reminded us that love has no limits. A neighbor is anyone who is in need. So don't look the other way. Don't just pass by. Do what you can to love God by loving those who are helpless and hopeless.

KEY IDEA

Love has no limits. Jews and Samaritans didn't exactly get along. It's easy to love someone who is like us. But Jesus teaches us to love all.

LET'S DISCUSS TOGETHER

- *Why should the first two men have helped?*
- *How did the Samaritan show mercy?*
- *What is one way you can help others in need?*

LET'S PRAY TOGETHER

Jesus, thank You for loving us. You laid down Your life for us, even before we loved You. Help us love others and love all with the same kind of love. In Jesus' name, amen.

• • • • • • •

For Further Study: Luke 10:25–37

72

FINDING WHAT IS LOST

• • • • • • • • •

"I tell you that in the same way there will be more rejoicing
in heaven over one sinner who repents than over ninety-nine
righteous persons who do not need to repent."

LUKE 15:7

Jesus found Himself in trouble once again. But not because He had
done something wrong. It was what the religious leaders thought He
was doing wrong—hanging out with sinners! Jesus had just invited a
"sinner," the tax collector Matthew, to come follow Him. So to make sure
they understood God's love, He told several parables about looking for
something that was lost.

"Suppose one of you had one hundred sheep and lost one. Would
you go after the one that was missing?" Jesus asked. "Or suppose one of
you had ten very expensive coins. What would you do if you lost one?
Wouldn't you go searching, looking everywhere until you found it?"

God doesn't want us to be like sinners; He wants us to love sinners.

Some people are lost because they want to be. They know about
God's love but aren't interested in believing in Him or loving Him. But
some people are lost because no one has gone looking for them. No one
has told them about what Jesus has done for them. They've never heard
about His love and forgiveness.

The religious leaders were waiting for sinners to come to them. Jesus went looking for sinners out of His love for them. He didn't want to wait; Jesus wanted to search! And guess what? He wants us to have the same heart for friends or family members who are lost. He wants to work through us, our family, and our church to seek and save people who are lost.

LET'S DISCUSS TOGETHER

- *In what ways does God search for people?*
- *How are people lost?*
- *Why is it important for us to live differently?*

LET'S PRAY TOGETHER

Heavenly Father, we are so grateful that You sent Jesus to search for us so He could save us. Show us those around us who need to know Your love. Work through us to search for those who are not following You yet. In Jesus' name, amen.

● ● ● ● ● ● ●

For Further Study: Matthew 18:12–14; Luke 15:1–10

73

THE LOST SON

• • • • • • • •

"'This son of mine was dead and is alive again; he was lost and is found.' So they began to celebrate."

LUKE 15:24

Y ou want me to do *what?*" the father asked his youngest son. "I want you to give me my inheritance *now*. Not someday when you die." The father was shocked and deeply saddened, but he gave his son what he wanted.

With the money in his hands, the son was out of there. He went to distant towns, met new people, and made a lot of bad choices. He also wasted all his money! Realizing the terrible mistakes he had made, he knew the only choice to make was to go home—back to his father, to the place where he belonged and where he was loved.

"I have wronged God and my father. I am not even worthy to be called his son," he said to himself. Off he went, toward home, hoping he could at least be a servant in his father's house. But when his father saw him, he ran. Picking up his speed, his father finally reached him. And when he did, he wrapped his arms around him, kissed him, and was filled with joy.

"I am so sorry," the son said to his father. "I have sinned against God and you."

Instead of punishing his son, this father threw a party for his son! But his other son wasn't so happy. "Haven't I always been here and obeyed you? Where is my party?" he complained.

"True," his father said, "but we had to celebrate and be glad because this brother of yours was dead and is alive again; he was lost and is found."

Jesus told this story to show how God our Father welcomes sinners. He rejoices over them when they come home, and so should we!

KEY IDEA

Only God satisfies. The youngest son was looking for happiness. The problem was that he was looking in all the wrong places! Only a relationship with God can truly satisfy our hearts.

LET'S DISCUSS TOGETHER

- *Why did Jesus tell this story to the religious leaders?*
- *What do you think the youngest son was searching for?*
- *How is coming back to God like coming home?*

LET'S PRAY TOGETHER

Heavenly Father, thank You for always loving us. You are patient and kind. Even when we sin, You don't stop caring for us. You always have open arms, willing to forgive us. In Jesus' name, amen.

• • • • • •

For Further Study: Luke 15:11–32

74

FIVE LOAVES OF BREAD AND TWO FISH

• • • • • • • • •

Jesus then took the loaves, gave thanks, and distributed to those who were seated as much as they wanted. He did the same with the fish.

JOHN 6:11

Their stomachs were growling. Five thousand people sat with empty bellies, waiting to be fed. But how? How could so many people, the disciples wondered, be satisfied when they didn't have any food to offer them? Seeing the crowds, the disciples panicked.

Philip said, "It would take more than half a year's wages to buy enough bread for each one to have a bite!" Andrew saw a boy sitting nearby. He had a few scraps—five loaves of bread and two fish. "Certainly, the boy's food is not enough to feed all of these people!" he said.

But with Jesus, all things are possible.

He took the boy's scraps of bread and fish, gave thanks to God the Father, and told His disciples to feed the crowd. One by one, each person ate. And they were full. Not only was everyone stuffed, but when the disciples collected the baskets of food, there were leftovers!

Once again Jesus proved who He was by performing a miracle. But it was a miracle He performed through an unlikely person.

Jesus chose a boy with just a few loaves of bread and two fish. It wasn't a lot, but it was enough. It always is with God. It is His work. His power. And He chooses to take what little we have sometimes and do something great with it!

What do you have? Is there something that seems small or insignificant to you? God can take whatever you have and multiply it. He took the boy's scraps and did a great miracle. He can do the same with what you offer Him.

LET'S DISCUSS TOGETHER

- *Why do you think the disciples still doubted Jesus?*
- *What do you think the boy's reaction was to Jesus' miracle?*
- *What is important for us to remember from this story?*

LET'S PRAY TOGETHER

Jesus, we give You what we have. You have blessed us with different gifts, abilities, and even possessions. Use them so others may see Your love and power. In Jesus' name, amen.

• • • • • • •

For Further Study: John 6:1–15

159

75

THE BREAD OF LIFE

• • • • • • • • •

Jesus declared, "I am the bread of life. Whoever comes to me will
never go hungry, and whoever believes in me will never be thirsty."
JOHN 6:35

What is your favorite food to eat? After you have eaten a good meal,
how long does it take for you to get hungry again? I'll bet not too
long. Jesus talked about a different kind of food. This food we can eat and
never get hungry again.

Shortly after Jesus fed the five thousand, He and His disciples got
into their boats and crossed the lake. It didn't take long for the crowds
to follow Him. They were looking for another miracle—and more food
to eat!

"Show us another sign," they said, "then we'll believe you really
are sent from God. Our relatives who followed Moses ate bread in the
wilderness!"

But Jesus told them about a different kind of food. Better bread.
Bread from heaven!

"It's true Moses gave your relatives bread in the wilderness when
they left Egypt," Jesus said. "But they got hungry again. Their stomachs
growled. And eventually they died."

Then Jesus surprised them. He said, "My Father has given you bread from heaven. I am the bread from heaven. If you believe in Me, you will never get hungry again! And you will be with Me forever."

Only Jesus can make us happy. He is the real bread, the Bread of Life, that satisfies our greatest hunger. And best of all, when we believe in Him, we can be sure that one day we will spend forever with Him in heaven!

LET'S DISCUSS TOGETHER

- *What is your favorite food, and why?*
- *How is Jesus like bread?*
- *What promise does Jesus give us if we believe in Him?*

LET'S PRAY TOGETHER

Heavenly Father, thank You for sending Jesus to be our Savior. He is the Bread of Life—the only One who can truly make us happy. Strengthen us with His truth and love. In Jesus' name, amen.

● ● ● ● ● ● ●

For Further Study: John 6:25–59

76
THE LIGHT OF THE WORLD

• • • • • • • • •

"I am the light of the world. Whoever follows me will never walk in darkness, but will have the light of life."

JOHN 8:12

Have you ever had the lights go out at your home? What did you do? Most likely, you lit a candle, grabbed a flashlight, or turned on a phone. The darkness can be scary. Darkness makes it hard to see and know where to go.

But the good news is, we don't have to stay in the dark.

One day when Jesus was at the temple teaching, He told the religious leaders something they didn't like. It confused them. It also left them with a choice. He said, "I am the light of the world. Whoever follows me will never walk in darkness, but will have the light of life" (John 8:12).

"Who are you to say you are the Light of the World?" they demanded to know. But Jesus didn't back down. He wanted everyone to know that following Him was like walking out of darkness and into light.

Jesus helps us see clearly who God is.

He helps us see clearly the way to live.

And Jesus, the Savior of the world, helps us see clearly the way to heaven.

We all have a choice to make—stay in the dark or follow the Light.

Jesus reminded us that we were all once in the dark. We didn't know God. We didn't know how to love Him or have a relationship with Him. But the true Light of the World appeared to us. And that has changed everything!

LET'S DISCUSS TOGETHER

- *What is so scary about darkness?*
- *How is Jesus like a light?*
- *What promise does Jesus make to us when it feels like we are walking in the dark?*

LET'S PRAY TOGETHER

Jesus, You are the Light of the World. You have saved us and given us peace and hope. You are the One who goes before us, lighting our path so we can see clearly. In Jesus' name, amen.

● ● ● ● ● ●

For Further Study: John 8:12–20

163

77

THE GOOD SHEPHERD

• • • • • • • • •

"I am the good shepherd. The good shepherd lays down his life for the sheep."

JOHN 10:11

Have you ever lost something really important to you? What did you do to find it? Jesus, when He was telling others about who He was, said He was like a shepherd who loves his sheep. He wasn't talking about animals though; He was talking about people!

Sometimes sheep get lost. They run in every direction. And they wander off. But other times sheep go their own way because they don't have anyone looking out for them. People are the same way. They need a shepherd. One who would do anything for them. This is why God the Father sent Jesus.

God's people had become like sheep without a shepherd. The religious leaders were supposed to be taking care of them, watching over them, teaching them, and partnering with what God was doing in the world.

So Jesus said to them, "I am the good shepherd. The good shepherd lays down his life for the sheep."

Like a good shepherd, He protects us. He leads us. Jesus cares for us. He feeds us with truth. He doesn't want us to wander off, get lost, or follow the wrong voice. He wants us to listen to His voice.

So who are you following? What voice do you listen to? Jesus is our Good Shepherd whom we can trust. We can follow Him. How do we know this? Because He died for us so we could be forgiven. He is the kind of Shepherd worth following!

LET'S DISCUSS TOGETHER

- *How do people get lost?*
- *What does Jesus say a good shepherd does for his sheep?*
- *How do we let Jesus lead us?*

LET'S PRAY TOGETHER

Heavenly Father, You have sent Jesus to save us, care for us, and guide us. He is the Good Shepherd who is always there to protect and provide for us. Help us follow Him, trusting that He knows what is best for us. In Jesus' name, amen.

• • • • • •

For Further Study: John 10:1–21

78

FOLLOWING THE RIGHT DIRECTIONS

• • • • • • • • •

Jesus answered, "I am the way and the truth and the life. No one comes to the Father except through me."

JOHN 14:6

Have you ever had to ask for directions? Maybe you were looking for someone's house or you were trying to find a store. Maybe you were on vacation and couldn't find the right street. Everyone can get lost. That's why we need to be careful to follow the right directions!

One day Jesus was telling His disciples about heaven. The Bible says it's going to be like everything Adam and Eve had but even better! Jesus told them it was like a house with many rooms. It is a place where God lives with us. It is a place where we are together again. There is no more pain, sickness, tears, war, or hunger.

And then Jesus told them He was going to leave them soon. But not forever. He was preparing a place for them, a place to belong, to finally be at home forever!

Who wouldn't want to go where Jesus was talking about! But how do we get there? That is the question the disciples wanted to know. They needed directions. And so do we.

Jesus told us He is the way, the truth, and the life. Coming to Him, believing in Him, and following Him is the *only* way to being with God forever! Jesus is not *a* way; He is *the* way. Like a road sign pointing us in the right direction, Jesus pointed us toward real life and everlasting life.

KEY IDEA

Jesus is not a way; Jesus is the way. Many people think that if they are good and try not to sin, God will accept them. But only Jesus can save us. Only by believing in what He has done for us on the cross will we be forgiven and accepted by God the Father. We can be sure that when we follow Jesus, we will be with Him forever.

LET'S DISCUSS TOGETHER

- *Describe a time when you had to ask for directions.*
- *What do you think is going to be the best part of heaven someday?*
- *How can people be sure they are heading in the right direction?*

LET'S PRAY TOGETHER

Heavenly Father, we praise You for saving us through Your Son, Jesus. He is the only way to heaven, the only way to You. Fill us with Your joy and hope, knowing that we are going to be with You forever someday. In Jesus' name, amen.

• • • • • • •

For Further Study: John 14:1–14

167

79

THE UNFORGIVING SERVANT

• • • • • • • • •

Peter came to Jesus and asked, "Lord, how many times shall I forgive my brother or sister who sins against me? Up to seven times?" Jesus answered, "I tell you, not seven times, but seventy-seven times."

MATTHEW 18:21-22

How many times should I forgive someone?" Peter asked Jesus. "Once? Twice? How about seven times?" Jesus gave a shocking answer. "Not seven, but seventy-seven times!" In other words, Jesus was saying we should always be willing to forgive.

Then He told a story about a servant who wouldn't forgive. This servant owed a huge debt to the king. When the king came to collect his money, the servant begged and pleaded. "Be patient with me," the servant cried. "I'll pay you back!" And the king showed him kindness and cancelled his debt.

The servant couldn't believe it. *I never could have paid all of that money back,* he thought to himself. But then something strange happened. He ran into a friend who owed him money. Not a lot of money. Just a little.

His friend begged and pleaded, "Be patient with me. I'll pay you back!" The servant would not forgive. He refused to cancel the debt. Instead, he had him thrown into prison.

Peter must have been amazed at the servant in Jesus' story. But he got the point: we should forgive because we have been forgiven of so much!

The next time you need to forgive someone, stop and think. Remember how much God has loved you by forgiving you. Forgive the way you have been forgiven!

KEY IDEA

Forgiving is refusing to get even. When someone does something we don't like, we might be tempted to try to get even. We might get mad, yell, or try to hurt them. But living for God requires living differently. As Christians, we overcome evil with good, choosing to forgive instead of getting even. We choose to love others the way God first loved us.

LET'S DISCUSS TOGETHER

- *How do some people treat others when they have been hurt?*
- *Why do you think Jesus' story was so shocking?*
- *What is one thing you can do to be more forgiving of others?*

LET'S PRAY TOGETHER

Heavenly Father, thank You for being patient with us. You always love us. You are quick to forgive when we sin against You. Give us Your power. Change our hearts so we are able to treat others the way You treat us. In Jesus' name, amen.

For Further Study: Matthew 18:21–35

80

THE UNUSUAL KING ARRIVES

• • • • • • • • •

Rejoice greatly, Daughter Zion! Shout, Daughter Jerusalem! See, your king comes to **you**, righteous and victorious, lowly and riding on a donkey, on a colt, the foal of a donkey.

ZECHARIAH 9:9

T he streets of Jerusalem were packed. It was Passover, a time when the Jewish people remembered their exodus out of Egypt. God had saved them from their enemies. But He was about to do something new—something better. A greater Deliverer was coming. This was the King of all kings, the Messiah God had spoken about for years through His prophets.

It was time for Jesus to reveal who He really was. He sent two of His disciples to get a donkey for him to ride into Jerusalem. There was a buzz in the air. Jesus could see and hear the crowds.

And then they spotted Him. *Surely He is coming to save Israel and get rid of the Romans!* The crowds swarmed toward Jesus. They began to wave palm branches. Then they shouted:

> "Hosanna to the Son of David!"
> "Blessed is he who comes in the name of the Lord!"
> "Hosanna in the highest heaven!" (Matthew 21:9)

But they didn't realize that the Savior would come twice. The first time, Jesus was coming as a suffering Servant to save them from an even greater Enemy than the Romans by dying on the cross. Jesus was coming to set them free from their sins. But He is also coming a second time as a powerful King—and that time He will change the world once and for all by bringing peace, love, and all that is good!

LET'S DISCUSS TOGETHER

- *What did the Jewish people think Jesus was coming to do?*
- *What was Jesus really coming to do?*
- *How is sin a greater enemy?*

LET'S PRAY TOGETHER

Heavenly Father, You have been faithful to send Your Savior to deliver us from the power of sin. Jesus is the real King who loves us and leads us. And one day we know He will come again to deliver us forever. In His name, amen.

• • • • • • •

For Further Study: Matthew 21:1–11; Mark 11:1–11; Luke 19:28–44; John 12:12–19

81

THE LAST SUPPER

• • • • • • • • •

Whenever you eat this bread and drink this cup, you proclaim the Lord's death until he comes.

1 CORINTHIANS 11:26

The candles on the table flickered in the darkness. There was a warm glow, splashing just enough light onto the faces of each of the disciples. Reclining at the table that night, their eyes looked eager. They had gathered in Jerusalem, but this seemed like a different kind of Passover meal.

They were right. This was no ordinary meal. This would be Jesus' last meal with them before going to the cross.

His words pierced their hearts when He told them that one of them would turn away from Him. "Not me, Jesus. I would never betray You!" Peter said. And then Jesus said something that stretched their minds but made their hearts begin to come alive. But they didn't fully understand what He meant at the time.

After He prayed, He took bread, broke it, and said, "This is My body. Take it and eat it." Then Jesus prayed again. He picked up a cup and said, "This is My blood. Drink it. I am making a new covenant with you."

Jesus was explaining that in a short time, He was going to die on the cross for the forgiveness of sins. His body would be broken and bruised for us. His blood would be shed. But it would mean life, new life, everlasting life for all who believed!

And then Jesus said, "From now on, do this. Eat and drink. Don't ever forget what I have done for you. One day we will eat and drink again when I return!"

KEY IDEA

Jesus died so we could live. As Jesus sat around the table with His disciples, He was teaching them that He was going to die for them. Still today, Christians remember this new covenant by taking communion or the Lord's Supper at their churches. Jesus said we should always do this until He returns; it is a way of remembering what God has done for us.

LET'S DISCUSS TOGETHER

- *Why did the disciples not fully understand what Jesus meant?*
- *What do the bread and cup represent?*
- *Why is remembering so important?*

LET'S PRAY TOGETHER

Heavenly Father, thank You for saving us through Your Son, Jesus. Help us not to forget. Help us remember just how much You love us. In Jesus' name, amen.

● ● ● ● ● ● ●

For Further Study: Matthew 26:17-30; Mark 14:12-26; Luke 22:7-38; John 13:1-17

82

A GRUELING NIGHT IN GETHSEMANE

• • • • • • • • •

"My Father, if it is not possible for this cup to be taken away unless I drink it, may your will be done."

MATTHEW 26:42

Have you ever had to do something you really didn't want to do? Something you knew was going to be incredibly hard? This is exactly what Jesus wrestled with one grueling night in the Garden of Gethsemane.

Darkness covered Jesus, along with Peter, James, and John. The hour was getting closer. Jesus needed to be alone with His heavenly Father.

"Sit here while I go over there and pray," Jesus told them. When He returned, He found them asleep! This happened not once but three times.

"Are you still sleeping and resting? Look, the hour has come, and the Son of Man is delivered into the hands of sinners. Rise! Let us go! Here comes my betrayer!" (Matthew 26:45–46).

Jesus was overcome with sorrow. He knew what He had to do. Some of His followers were about to betray and disown Him. He would be arrested. But Jesus had come to do His Father's will.

Talking about His death, Jesus prayed, "Father, if it is possible, take this cup. But if I must drink it, then I will do it. I will obey You. Not My will be done, but Your will be done."

Jesus knew His Father's heart, so He obeyed His Father's will. Following God will not always be easy. It might be hard and confusing. But we can always trust God's heart: He is good and faithful and true. Listening to God is always the best thing, even if it's not the easiest thing.

KEY IDEA

Jesus knew His Father's heart, so He obeyed His Father's will. When we know that God is good and wants what is best for us, we can trust and obey Him. He's not trying to ruin our life; He is trying to give us life!

LET'S DISCUSS TOGETHER

- *How do you think Jesus felt when the disciples fell asleep?*
- *How would you describe God's heart, and why is this important when obeying God?*
- *Is there one area in your life in which it's hard to do what God wants?*

LET'S PRAY TOGETHER

Heavenly Father, give us hearts that are willing to listen and obey You. Help us trust You. We want to live like Jesus and say, "Not my will be done, but Your will be done." In Jesus' name, amen.

● ● ● ● ● ● ● ●

For Further Study: Matthew 26:36–68; Mark 14:32–65; Luke 22:39–53

83

COSTLY LOVE

• • • • • • • • •

This is how we know what love is: Jesus Christ laid down his life for us. And we ought to lay down our lives for our brothers and sisters.

1 JOHN 3:16

Angry soldiers and a large crowd surrounded Jesus. They took Him to Caiaphas, the high priest. The religious leaders wanted Jesus dead. They were furious He had claimed to be God's Son, the promised Messiah.

When Pilate, the Roman governor, asked if He was the King of the Jews, Jesus simply said, "You have said so" (Matthew 27:11). He had done no wrong. He'd never sinned. He was pure and perfect love being poured out for all.

But the crowds shouted anyway: "Crucify him! Crucify him!" (Luke 23:21). The soldiers mocked Him. When He was beaten and bruised, they put a piercing crown of thorns on His head. They made Him carry His cross through winding streets, all the way to Golgotha, which means "the place of the skull" (Matthew 27:33). And then they nailed Him to the cross—between two thieves.

The weight of the world's sin was on Him. He felt the presence of His Father pull away. With one final blast of breath, He cried out, "It is finished!" (John 19:30). It was not a cry of defeat; it was a shout of victory.

He had done His Father's will. He took our place, was punished for our sin. He had paid the penalty we deserve. Now forgiveness and salvation were available for all.

What a costly and beautiful love: a love willing to sacrifice—a love willing to do what is best for someone else. This kind of love is what we are called to carry into a hurting world!

KEY IDEA

Jesus paid the punishment we deserve. Our sin separates us from God. And because God is just, it must be punished. But out of love, Jesus took our place on the cross. He suffered not for His sin but for ours. Instead of being punished for our sin, we are forgiven of our sin!

LET'S DISCUSS TOGETHER

- *Why were the religious leaders upset with Jesus?*
- *Why did Jesus cry out, "It is finished"?*
- *What is one way to sacrificially love someone else?*

LET'S PRAY TOGETHER

Heavenly Father, thank You for not treating us like we deserve because of our sins. Instead of punishing us, You have forgiven us through Your Son, Jesus. Help us love others with the same costly love. In Jesus' name, amen.

● ● ● ● ● ● ● ● ●

For Further Study: Matthew 27:11–44; Mark 15:1–32; Luke 23:1–49; John 19:1–37

84

HE IS RISEN

• • • • • • • • •

He is not here; he has risen, just as he said. Come and see the place where he lay.

MATTHEW 28:6

I t looked like all hope was lost. Everything God had promised, every-thing God had been doing, all seemed to be over. Was it all a mistake? Had Jesus' followers believed a lie?

Taking Jesus' body, a man named Joseph wrapped Him in a cloth then placed Him in a cave used for a grave. Afraid the disciples would try to steal Jesus' body and tell everyone He was risen, the Romans rolled a large stone in front of Jesus' grave and sealed it. Then they placed guards in front of it.

But this was no match for heaven. No match for God's work in the world. God was far from done! On the third day, two women came to visit the grave.

The earth began to shake. An angel of the Lord appeared and rolled the stone away. Light exploded in every direction. "I know you are look-ing for Jesus," the angel said. "He was crucified, buried, and now risen! Look, He is not here!"

The angel told the women to go get the word out. Go tell the disciples. Death had been defeated!

Filled with inexpressible joy, they ran toward Galilee. They couldn't wait to tell the disciples. But on the way, Jesus stopped them in their tracks.

"Greetings," He said. "Go tell My disciples I am coming to see them."

It was all true! So they fell at Jesus' feet and worshipped Him. Jesus is alive. His victory is our victory! Life has conquered death, and one day we will be with Him forever.

KEY IDEA

Jesus' victory is our victory. When Jesus died, some wondered if He really was who He claimed to be. His resurrection proved it. His resurrection gives us the hope that one day we will be with Him forever.

LET'S DISCUSS TOGETHER

- *Why is it impossible that the disciples stole Jesus' body?*
- *How did Jesus' resurrection prove who He was?*
- *Why does Jesus' resurrection give us hope?*

LET'S PRAY TOGETHER

Heavenly Father, we praise You for the hope we have in Jesus. Not only did He die for us, but You raised Him from the dead. Thank You that we can be sure that one day we too will be with You forever. In Jesus' name, amen.

• • • • • • •

For Further Study: Matthew 27:57–28:15; Mark 15:42–47; Luke 24:1–35

85

PEACE BE WITH YOU

• • • • • • • • •

Jesus came and stood among them and said, "Peace be with you!"
JOHN 20:19

The disciples were terrified. Locked in a room, they were afraid of what the Jewish leaders might do to them. And so they hid. They had heard that Jesus was alive again, but He had not yet appeared to them. Fear, not faith, gripped them.

But suddenly Jesus showed up—right inside the locked room. With love in His eyes, He comforted them and said, "Peace be with you!"

The disciples couldn't believe their eyes! Hope was not lost. Life had conquered death. And if that wasn't enough, Jesus showed them the scars on His hands and His side. "Touch them," Jesus said. "Don't doubt, but have faith!"

Then He said, "Receive the Holy Spirit," reminding them and preparing them for the gift He would give them at Pentecost, along with all Christians when they believe in Him.

In a flash, their fear vanished. Jesus really is who He claimed to be. Instead of being filled with fear, they were filled with faith. With God's help, they now had peace, courage, and devotion.

Then Jesus reminded them that there was much work to be done.

Just as God the Father had sent Him, He was now sending them into the world.

"Go share the good news. Let the world know what God's amazing love and forgiveness look like. Make more disciples, baptizing them in the name of the Father, Son, and Holy Spirit. And teach them to obey everything I have commanded you."

Just as Jesus had to remind His disciples, He reminds us today: *Don't be afraid. Don't doubt. Believe. I am always with you and working through you!*

KEY IDEA

God's power is our power. When we believe in Jesus, God the Father gives us the gift of the Holy Spirit to live in us. It is His presence and power, not our own strength, that helps us live for God.

LET'S DISCUSS TOGETHER

- *Why were the disciples so afraid?*
- *What gave the disciples courage?*
- *How can fear keep us from living for God?*

LET'S PRAY TOGETHER

Heavenly Father, help us not be fearful. Give us faith. Make us confident. Just like the disciples, give us the courage to be devoted to You. In Jesus' name, amen.

● ● ● ● ● ● ●

For Further Study: Matthew 28:16–20; Luke 24:36–49; John 20:19–29

86

PURPOSE AND POWER

· · · · · · · · · ·

"You will receive power when the Holy Spirit comes on you;
and you will be my witnesses in Jerusalem, and in all Judea and
Samaria, and to the ends of the earth."

ACTS 1:8

What does it mean to have a purpose? Shortly after Jesus' resurrection, He appeared to His disciples. For more than forty days, He spent time with them. He taught them, encouraged them, and gave them even more proof that He really was alive. And He gave them a purpose—a mission.

One day, when Jesus was eating with His disciples, He said, "Stay here in Jerusalem. In just a few days you will receive power when the Holy Spirit comes on you; and you will be my witnesses in Jerusalem, and in all Judea and Samaria, and to the ends of the earth."

Then, like a king going up to his throne, Jesus ascended into heaven. The disciples were stunned. Their eyes were wide open. Staring up at the sky, they suddenly heard the sound of a voice: "Men of Galilee, just as your eyes saw Jesus leave, your eyes will see Him return one day."

He was gone. But He had not left them alone. Jesus had been crucified, resurrected, and now is reigning like a King in heaven! He is with us through the power of the Holy Spirit. The purpose He gave His disciples nearly two thousand years ago is the same purpose we have today.

God has made each of us unique. We have different gifts and abilities. Each of us lives in a different place, surrounded by different people. But we all have the same purpose—to be witnesses for Jesus.

LET'S DISCUSS TOGETHER

- *What does it mean to be a witness?*
- *What power does God give us to be witnesses?*
- *Who is one person you can be a witness to?*

LET'S PRAY TOGETHER

Heavenly Father, You have given us a purpose. Help us be witnesses for Jesus to the people You have surrounded us with. Help them see Jesus in us. In Jesus' name, amen.

• • • • • • •

For Further Study: Acts 1:1–11

183

87

THE DANGER OF INDIFFERENCE

• • • • • • • • •

Peter replied, "Repent and be baptized, every one of you, in the name of Jesus Christ for the forgiveness of your sins. And you will receive the gift of the Holy Spirit."

ACTS 2:38

I t felt like an explosion. A rushing wind blew through the room the disciples were sitting in. What looked like tongues of fire rested on each of them. Just as Jesus had promised, they were filled with the gift of the Holy Spirit.

Thousands and thousands of people were in Jerusalem celebrating Pentecost, an important holiday for the Jewish people. Men and women from many different nations were there, along with their children. Little did they know, they were about to hear the best news of their lives! That news would require them to make a decision.

When the disciples were filled with the Holy Spirit, they were each miraculously able to speak in a different language. Why? So everyone gathered in Jerusalem could hear and understand the good news about Jesus in their own language!

Peter stood up and preached without fear. "Turn from your sins and turn to Jesus," he said. "God wants to forgive you and give you new life. And be baptized; God wants you to be a part of His family!"

Some people laughed. They made fun of the disciples. Others walked away. But others' hearts were softened by God's love. They believed, turned from their sins, and were baptized.

That day, the church was born. It all started with three thousand people making a decision to follow Jesus.

Devotion to Jesus always requires a decision about Jesus. What have you decided about Jesus?

KEY IDEA

The church is the body of Christ. Acts 2 describes the very beginning of the church. All who believe in Jesus and are filled with the Holy Spirit are a part of the church, sometimes called the body of Christ. Church isn't just a place we go to on Sunday; church is like a family we belong to. We are all brothers and sisters in Christ!

LET'S DISCUSS TOGETHER

- *What does it mean to repent?*
- *How should we let Jesus lead our lives?*
- *What is one way to show devotion to Jesus?*

LET'S PRAY TOGETHER

Heavenly Father, thank You that we belong to Your family, the church. Be the center of our lives, teaching us to follow You with all our hearts. In Jesus' name, amen.

● ● ● ● ● ● ●

For Further Study: Acts 2:1-41

88

BETTER TOGETHER

· · · · · · · · ·

All the believers were together and had everything in common.

ACTS 2:44

How would you describe your closest friendships? What makes them different from other relationships? As Jesus' new church was growing, the people were also growing closer together. Church was not just going to a service once a week or singing a few worship songs. It was like a family—a place to believe and belong.

Daily, they followed Jesus. Loving one another. Serving one another. Telling others about God's love. Jesus was at the center of not just one day but every day!

In Acts 2, we're told that the new believers continued to go to the temple courts to worship God, but they also met together in people's homes. They devoted themselves to studying God's Word. They ate together and celebrated the Lord's Supper. Praying together often, they saw God do amazing things in their lives!

And when someone had a need, they helped each other. Sometimes they even sold their own stuff to help another Christian in need. They had "everything in common." They were one. Undivided.

People noticed something was different about the church. They had a kind of love and concern for one another that others didn't. They didn't treat each other like strangers; they treated each other like family. So people wanted to belong to the church, and they wanted to believe in Jesus.

The world was watching, and it made a difference. In fact, "the Lord added to their number daily those who were being saved" (Acts 2:47). Our lives really do matter. People are watching. How does your love make someone else want to belong to God's amazing family, the church?

KEY IDEA

We are better together. Living for Jesus isn't something we do alone. God has brought us into a new family: the church. God uses other people to help us, encourage us, and grow us. We become more like Jesus together.

LET'S DISCUSS TOGETHER

- *How is belonging to a church different from just going to church?*
- *What was so different about the early church?*
- *What is one way you can make your church feel more like a family?*

LET'S PRAY TOGETHER

Heavenly Father, thank You for the gift of other people. You have given us a new family, the church. We not only believe in You, but we belong to one another. Continue to teach us, grow us, and draw us closer together. In Jesus' name, amen.

• • • • • • •

For Further Study: Acts 2:42–47

89

COURAGEOUS FAITH

• • • • • • • •

As for us, we cannot help speaking about what we have seen and heard.

ACTS 4:20

Having courage doesn't mean you don't have fear. It means you still act. You overcome your fear by stepping out in faith to do what God wants you to do—no matter how you feel!

Not everyone was happy the church was growing so fast. Many of the Jewish religious leaders wanted the disciples to stop and keep this message about Jesus to themselves. But they wouldn't.

One day Peter and John were proclaiming the good news about Jesus. "He is the Savior the prophets told us about. He died and has risen again," they said. A group of religious leaders had had enough. They had Peter and John thrown into prison. *That will keep them quiet*, they thought.

"We won't stop. We won't keep quiet. After all God has done for us, how could we? We cannot help speaking about what we have seen and heard," they said.

"Salvation is found in no one else, for there is no other name under heaven given to mankind by which we must be saved" (Acts 4:12).

This really made the religious leaders mad. But that didn't matter to Peter and John. They were more concerned about pleasing God than pleasing people. The Holy Spirit gave them courage, boldness, a faith that burned like a fire in them.

Not everyone we meet will be happy about our faith in Jesus. Just as it took courage for the disciples to follow Jesus, it takes courage for us too. We need to be bold and unafraid about what others think. How do you need more courage?

KEY IDEA

It's better to please God than please people.
It can be hard to be a Christian. Sometimes people might make fun of you or they might treat you differently. But don't worry. There is no need to be embarrassed or scared. What God thinks about us is far more important!

LET'S DISCUSS TOGETHER

- *Describe a time when you were fearful to do something.*
- *Why do we need to have courage to follow Jesus?*
- *What is one way to be bold with our faith?*

LET'S PRAY TOGETHER

Heavenly Father, give us courage. Fill us with Your Holy Spirit. When we feel scared, give us strength to please You more than we please people. We want to walk in faith and not fear. In Jesus' name, amen.

• • • • • •

For Further Study: Acts 4:1-22

90

THE POWER OF PRAYER

• • • • • • • • •

After they prayed, the place where they were meeting was shaken. And they were all filled with the Holy Spirit and spoke the word of God boldly.

ACTS 4:31

What do you usually pray for? Do you pray for what you want or need? As the church was continuing to grow, we see another kind of prayer. We might call it a God-centered prayer—a prayer that is focused on what God wants and is doing.

Once again, the disciples gathered in a room together. Peter and John told everyone what had just happened, how the religious leaders wanted them to stop talking about the good news of Jesus. They told them about the threats and warnings. Instead of giving up, hiding, or running away, they prayed.

"Lord, You are the Creator and Maker of heaven and earth. Anything is possible with You. You sent Jesus to save us from our sins. Give us strength. Help us to be bold!" they prayed.

And God heard their prayers. The room they were staying in shook. God filled them with His Spirit. Giving them boldness, God continued to work through them in new and exciting ways!

God works where He is welcome. By crying out to God, the disciples were welcoming God to continue working in them and through them.

How are you welcoming God to work through you? Maybe in your school. Your neighborhood. A friend or family member. What would you love to see Him do? Just like the disciples, pray about it. And watch how God shows up!

KEY IDEA

There is power in prayer. The Bible tells us that the Lord hears our prayers. God is a Father who loves us and listens to us. He is full of power, wisdom, and love. He wants us to come to Him. Our prayers are a way for God to change us and work through us.

LET'S DISCUSS TOGETHER

- *What is a God-centered prayer?*
- *How is prayer a way of welcoming God to work?*
- *What is one way you could pray differently?*

LET'S PRAY TOGETHER

Heavenly Father, we know You hear us and love us. We welcome You to come and work through us. Give us power and wisdom to be the kind of people You want us to be. In Jesus' name, amen.

• • • • • •

For Further Study: Acts 4:23-31

91

AMAZING GRACE

• • • • • • • • •

Here is a trustworthy saying that deserves full acceptance: Christ
Jesus came into the world to save sinners—of whom I am the worst.

1 TIMOTHY 1:15

Saul is about the last person you would expect to become a Christian. He was angry. An enemy of the church. A persecutor of the disciples. But he was not too bad of a sinner that God's grace couldn't save him!

One day Saul was on his way to find Christians. His plan was to take them back to Jerusalem and throw them in jail. But God had another plan.

On his way to the city of Damascus, suddenly a light from heaven flashed around him. He fell to the ground and heard a voice say to him, "Saul, Saul, why do you persecute me?"

"Who are you, Lord?" Saul asked. "I am Jesus, whom you are persecuting. . . . Now get up and go into the city, and you will be told what you must do" (Acts 9:5–6).

For three days, Saul was blind. Everything was pitch black. But the Lord told a man named Ananias to go to Damascus, place his hands on him, and pray so Saul could see again. Sure enough, it was like scales fell from Saul's eyes.

For the first time, Saul could *really* see. He saw his own sin. He saw his need to be forgiven. And he saw Jesus—not as an enemy but as his

Savior and Friend! God filled him with His Spirit, and Saul eventually became one of the church's greatest leaders and missionaries. Even his name would change—no longer Saul, he would be called Paul.

God's grace is amazing—far greater than sin! How do you see Jesus? Do you see Him as someone who wants to give you a real life and a good future?

KEY IDEA

God has a better future for us when we follow Him. Saul is a good example of how no one is too much of a sinner that they can't be saved by Jesus. Jesus didn't hold his past against him. He loved him, forgave him, and offered him a much better future.

LET'S DISCUSS TOGETHER

- *Do you know someone whom you think would never become a Christian?*
- *Why was Saul an unlikely follower of Jesus?*
- *How can you show love to someone you know who is like Saul?*

LET'S PRAY TOGETHER

Heavenly Father, You have treated us better than we deserve. Your grace is amazing. Thank You for loving us and forgiving us. You have good plans for us as we trust and obey You. In Jesus' name, amen.

• • • • • •

For Further Study: Acts 9:1–19

92

DON'T LET DIFFERENCES DIVIDE

• • • • • • • • •

There is neither Jew nor Gentile, neither slave nor free, nor is there
male and female, for you are all one in Christ Jesus.

GALATIANS 3:28

Have you ever had to love someone who was different from you?
Why was it hard? As the church was growing and spreading, different kinds of people were believing in Jesus. The disciples were running
into a problem. Some of their differences were dividing them.

God had a bigger plan than they realized—a bigger family.

It took a vision from God for the disciples to understand. God had to
speak to Peter and the leaders of the early church to help them see that
Jesus wasn't just the Savior for the Jewish people; He was the Savior for
all people. God played no favorites!

"We can't eat with them," some of the Christians who were Jewish
were saying. "They are Gentiles. They aren't Jewish like us. Surely they
aren't a part of God's family!" But they were wrong.

Just as many of the Jewish people were believing in Jesus and receiving the Holy Spirit, so were Gentiles. God was breaking down walls and
bringing people together who were different. Both Jews and Gentiles
needed to believe in Jesus. And when they did, they became one family.
One people. The church.

Our differences shouldn't divide us! We might look different, come from different countries, or speak different languages. We might have different pasts. But if we are followers of Jesus, we are one. We should treat one another like brothers and sisters. If God doesn't play favorites, we shouldn't either!

LET'S DISCUSS TOGETHER

- *Why can it be hard to love someone who is different?*
- *What does it mean to show favoritism toward someone else?*
- *What is one way you can love someone who is different?*

LET'S PRAY TOGETHER

Heavenly Father, thank You that You love each of us the same. You treat us as Your own. Teach us to love one another no matter what our differences are. Help us honor one another, showing kindness and respect. In Jesus' name, amen.

• • • • • • •

For Further Study: Acts 10–11

93

NOTHING IS IMPOSSIBLE

· · · · · · · · ·

Peter was kept in prison, but the church was earnestly praying to
God for him.

ACTS 12:5

Have you ever been in a situation that seemed impossible to get out
of? Where you thought it was a lost cause, with no way out? Peter
was too.

He had been out sharing the good news of Jesus' death and resurrection when King Herod's soldiers arrested him. "Enough!" Herod said,
"Have him thrown in prison!" So they locked Peter up, chaining him
nice and tight. Then placed one soldier on his right and one on his left.
Just in case, they even put a guard at the entrance of Peter's jail cell!

Peter was in an impossible situation.

How am I going to get out of here? he must have thought to himself.
I am in real trouble. I am never going to be free. But a group of friends,
followers of Jesus, began to pray. They prayed hard, crying out to God
for help.

That night, as Peter was sandwiched between two soldiers, the Lord
came to Peter's rescue. He sent an angel to set Peter free. The angel struck
Peter on the side and woke him up. "Quick, get up!" he said, and the
chains fell off Peter's wrists.

Peter couldn't believe his eyes. And neither could his friends when he arrived at their house. "It's Peter!" they yelled. "The Lord has done what we thought was impossible."

Nothing is too hard for our God. With His help, there is always a way out. He is our Rescuer, our Defender. When you feel scared, alone, or overwhelmed, remember that God is able to do all things.

KEY IDEA

With God, all things are possible. We don't always know what God's purposes are. Remember Joseph in the Old Testament? He was in prison for several years. But Peter's story reminds us we should always believe that God is powerful enough to rescue us from any situation. Don't lose heart. Keep praying and trusting God no matter what.

LET'S DISCUSS TOGETHER

- *Describe a time when you felt overwhelmed.*
- *How does God grow our faith when we are in impossible situations?*
- *Who is someone in a difficult situation whom you can pray for?*

LET'S PRAY TOGETHER

Lord, You are our strength. You are our Rescuer and Deliverer. Help us when we are afraid, and come to our defense when we are in need. In Jesus' name, amen.

● ● ● ● ● ● ●

For Further Study: Acts 12:1–19

197

94

ONE TRUE GOD

• • • • • • • • •

As I walked around and looked carefully at your objects of worship,
I even found an altar with this inscription: TO AN UNKNOWN GOD. So you
are ignorant of the very thing you worship.

ACTS 17:23

The apostle Paul couldn't believe his eyes. He, along with the other apostles, had been traveling to different cities. They were preaching the good news that Jesus had risen. But this city was different.

Athens was a very important city in Greece. It was large and full of people. It was a favorite spot for artists and philosophers, people who like to debate different ideas. It was also the perfect place to take the good news about Jesus' death and resurrection.

People were everywhere, and so were idols. Some were made of wood. Others were made out of stone. Step by step, Paul walked around the city, his eyes wide open. Finally, he couldn't keep quiet any longer.

"People of Athens! I see that in every way you are very religious. For as I walked around and looked carefully at your objects of worship, I even found an altar with this inscription: TO AN UNKNOWN GOD" (Acts 17:22–23).

The people of Athens were searching. Their hearts were restless. They knew there was something missing. So Paul explained to them that what they really needed was a relationship with the one true God, Jesus. Everything else is an idol, a false god. "Turn from your sins and turn to Jesus," he told them, "then you will find what you are really looking for!"

While many people don't worship stone statues anymore, an idol can be anything we make more important than our relationship with Jesus. It could be sports. Video games. A friendship. But only knowing and serving Jesus can truly make us happy.

KEY IDEA

An idol is a substitute for the one true God. Have you ever had a substitute teacher at school? Substitute teachers fill in, or take the place of, your real teacher. In the same way, idols take the place of our relationship with Jesus. They are not the real thing.

LET'S DISCUSS TOGETHER

- *What are common idols today?*
- *How do we sometimes make other things more important than God?*
- *Why will idols never make us happy like God can?*

LET'S PRAY TOGETHER

Dear Lord, only You can make us happy. Nothing can give us the joy, love, peace, and hope that a relationship with You can. Help us keep You at the center of our lives. In Jesus' name, amen.

• • • • • • •

For Further Study: Acts 17:16-34

95

TRUSTING WHAT GOD SAYS

· · · · · · · · ·

I urge you to keep up your courage, because not one of you will be lost; only the ship will be destroyed.

ACTS 27:22

The apostle Paul had a bad feeling about what he was about to do. It didn't seem safe. Having been arrested for telling others about Jesus, he was put on a ship to stand trial before Caesar in Rome.

"This is not going to go well," he told the crew. "We are going to suffer a great loss."

Sure enough, Paul was right. Swirling winds and crashing waves were about to destroy the ship. It would not be an easy journey to Rome. Everyone on board was terrified. Except for Paul.

Standing up, he said, "You should have listened to me! The ship will be destroyed. But don't be scared. God sent an angel to me last night and told me we are going to be okay." Encouraging them, he said, "So keep up your courage, men, for I have faith in God that it will happen *just as he told me*" (Acts 27:25).

How did Paul keep his faith in the storm? Was it how he felt? The storm was real. It was scary and dangerous. But what made Paul's heart calm was his confidence in what God had said.

All of us go through different "storms" in life. We might feel alone.

Thinking God is far from us, we might feel scared. But like Paul, our faith should come from what we know God says in His Word more than what we feel in our storms.

God has given us many truths about who He is. The Bible is full of amazing promises. When you find yourself in a storm, trust what God says and not just how you feel.

LET'S DISCUSS TOGETHER

- *Why should we be careful of basing our faith on our feelings?*
- *How do we base our faith on what God says?*
- *What is one way you can begin to know and remember what God says?*

LET'S PRAY TOGETHER

Heavenly Father, no matter what storms come our way, we can trust You. You are with us, giving us courage and hope. Increase our faith and help us to always look to You for our comfort and strength. In Jesus' name, amen.

• • • • • •

For Further Study: Acts 27

96

GO, GATHER, GROW

• • • • • • • • •

Let us consider how we may spur one another on toward love and good deeds, not giving up meeting together, as some are in the habit of doing, but encouraging one another—and all the more as you see the Day approaching.

HEBREWS 10:24-25

As more and more people began to follow Jesus, churches started to spring up one after another. At first these churches met in people's homes and later in their own buildings. But for every Christian, church was a place to go, gather, and grow!

Christians would study the Scriptures, along with the writings of the apostles (which eventually became what we call the New Testament). They would pray together. Sing praise songs. Celebrate communion or the Lord's Supper. And serve one another with the gifts God had given them. Does this sound like your church?

The writer of the book of Hebrews told a group of Jesus' followers to keep going to church. And keep growing. We need each other if we are going to keep growing in our faith and becoming more like Jesus.

Some Christians must have thought church was optional or not that important. Maybe they had become too busy doing other things. "One day, Jesus is going to return," the writer said. "Until He does, keep encouraging one another to love God and love others."

We can't love Jesus and not love His church.

It's a good reminder for us too, isn't it? Churches come in all different sizes. We meet in different places. We might have different styles. But they are all about Jesus, who is in charge of every Christian church. He loves His church and He wants us to love it too! So keep going, gathering, and growing.

KEY IDEA

We are better together. Jesus never wanted us to follow Him alone, which is why He gave us the church. We need each other to continue to grow in our faith. And you are never too young to help others grow too.

LET'S DISCUSS TOGETHER

- *Why is going to church so important?*
- *Instead of just going, how can you go to grow?*
- *Who is one person you can invite to go to church with you?*

LET'S PRAY TOGETHER

Heavenly Father, thank You for the gift of our church. We praise You for those at our church who help us grow closer to You. Help us remember how important it is to go, gather, and grow. In Jesus' name, amen.

● ● ● ● ● ●

For Further Study: Hebrews 10:23–25; 1 Corinthians 12

97

ROOTS AND FRUITS

· · · · · · · · ·

The fruit of the Spirit is love, joy, peace, forbearance, kindness, goodness, faithfulness, gentleness, and self-control. Against such things there is no law.

GALATIANS 5:22-23

How have you changed recently? What did you change and why? Some changes can be bad. Others can be good. But as we follow Jesus, God is the One changing us—and He is always changing us for the better!

One day as followers of Jesus were gathering for church, someone stood up and read a letter from Paul. Paul was writing to teach them what Jesus wanted them to be like. How He wanted them to live differently in the world.

"Don't live like you used to before you were a Christian! Remember how you used to be selfish, full of pride, always arguing, and never happy? Live differently! Let God change you—you should be controlled by the Holy Spirit, who lives in you," Paul said.

"The fruit of the Sprit is love, joy, peace, patience, kindness, goodness, faithfulness, gentleness, and self-control." *This* is how people should know you. And this is how people should know you belong to Jesus!

But how do we grow the fruit of the Spirit? The good news is that we don't change ourselves. God changes us!

First, and most importantly, we need to trust in Jesus. When we do, God gives us His Spirit to live in us. The Holy Spirit helps us grow, change, and become more like Jesus. Then, as we read the Bible, pray, go to church, serve others, and continue to say *yes* to living for Jesus, we start to bear good fruit—fruit of the Spirit!

KEY IDEA

We need good roots to bear good fruit. Just as a plant needs good roots, we do too so we can bear good fruit. We need to sink our life, like roots, into God's Word. We need to choose the right friends. And stay connected to God through worship and prayer. These are just some of the ways God changes us through the power of His Spirit.

LET'S DISCUSS TOGETHER

- *How does God change us?*
- *Which fruits of the Spirit do you need to ask for God's help with?*
- *What is one way you can allow the Holy Spirit to change you?*

LET'S PRAY TOGETHER

Heavenly Father, we open our hearts to the gift of Your Holy Spirit. Fill us and help us grow to be more like Jesus. We give You control. We say yes to You. In Jesus' name, amen.

● ● ● ● ● ● ●

For Further Study: Galatians 5:13–26

98

USING OUR WORDS WISELY

• • • • • • • • •

Do not let any unwholesome talk come out of your mouths, but only what is helpful for building others up according to their needs, that it may benefit those who listen.

EPHESIANS 4:29

Every day we use words. Thousands and thousands of words! We use words to tell people what we want. How we feel. And what we think. But what kind of words do we use? Do our words help others or hurt others?

Words are powerful. So powerful that when the apostle Paul was writing to a church in the city of Ephesus, he took time to remind them that following Jesus includes using words wisely.

"Don't let any unwholesome talk come out of your mouths," he said. "Build others up according to their needs, that it may benefit those who listen."

First, he told them what *not* to do! Don't let any "unwholesome talk come out of your mouths," Paul said. And then he told them what kind of words to use. Our words should "build others up," not tear them down. They should be helpful or good for those who are around us.

Instead of being rude, we should speak kindly. Instead of being critical, we can encourage. Don't gossip, which means to talk about other people when they aren't around. Instead of being disrespectful, we can honor one another. And we should speak the truth in love.

Remember that your words have power. They have the power to help or to hurt. So choose life with your words today. Use your words to encourage someone. Give a compliment. Text a friend a Bible verse. As Jesus-followers, our words matter. So use them wisely!

KEY IDEA

Words may hurt, but they have the power to help. Proverbs 18:21 says that the "tongue has the power of life and death." Choose your words carefully, and see how God uses them to work in someone's life.

LET'S DISCUSS TOGETHER

- *What is "unwholesome talk"?*
- *Where do you struggle with your words the most right now?*
- *What is one way you can "benefit" a friend or family member with your words?*

LET'S PRAY TOGETHER

Heavenly Father, help us use our words to build others up. Guard our lips from being critical, sarcastic, and unkind. Instead, teach us to bless and encourage others with what we say and how we say it. In Jesus' name, amen.

• • • • • • • •

For Further Study: Ephesians 4:17–32

99

STAND STRONG

• • • • • • • • •

Be strong in the Lord and in his mighty power. Put on the full armor of God, so that you can take your stand against the devil's schemes.

EPHESIANS 6:10–11

The Christian life is like a battle. But the weapons we use aren't like the world's weapons. We don't use guns or bombs. God has given us spiritual weapons to stand strong. To win the spiritual battle until Jesus returns.

Satan knew God was powerful and that God wanted to use His creation to tell the whole world what He was like. This is why he first tempted Adam and Eve in the garden. He wanted to stop God's plan from the very beginning. And now Satan knows the end of God's plan is coming soon.

His time is short. So he wants to do anything he can to destroy God's work in the world and keep people from their friendship with God.

When Paul was writing one of his letters to a church, he told them how to fight. How to stand strong. This is the way you resist the Devil's work: just as a soldier puts on armor to go to battle, a Christian puts on the armor of God.

Put on the belt of truth, filling your mind with God's Word. Keep Jesus close to your heart by putting on the breastplate of righteousness.

Wear the sandals of peace so you are ready to go where Jesus leads you. Guard your mind from Satan's lies by using the shield of faith and wearing the helmet of salvation. Pray always. And use the Sword of the Spirit, the Bible, to stay close to God.

Soldiers don't go into battle without armor; neither should we! Be alert. Put on your armor. Stand strong. God has given us everything we need to live for Him.

KEY IDEA

Greater is He who is in us than he that is in the world. The Bible tells us that the strength God gives us is stronger than our Enemy's attacks. Don't rely on your own strength; rely on the Holy Spirit, who lives in you. And put on God's armor so you are well prepared and protected!

LET'S DISCUSS TOGETHER

- *What piece of armor do you wear the most?*
- *What piece of armor do you need to wear more often?*
- *How or where are you most tempted by the "devil's schemes"?*

LET'S PRAY TOGETHER

Dear Lord, keep us strong. Protect us from our spiritual Enemy. Help us be wise, relying on the armor You give us to overcome temptation. In Jesus' name, amen.

• • • • • • • • •

For Further Study: Ephesians 6:10–20

100

A NEW HEAVEN AND A NEW EARTH

• • • • • • • • •

He who was seated on the throne said, "I am making everything new!" Then he said, "Write this down, for these words are trustworthy and true."

REVELATION 21:5

Everything that is wrong with the world is going to be made right one day. All the hurt. The brokenness. The pain. It's going to be fixed when God makes everything *new*!

This is the picture, the dream, that Jesus gave John. John was one of Jesus' oldest followers, and he was living on an island called Patmos. He had been sent there as punishment for telling others about Jesus. But there Jesus showed John an amazing picture—a dream, God's dream for His creation.

He saw Jesus dressed like a Warrior, riding a horse. He saw Satan being defeated once and for all. He saw a big and beautiful city, the New Jerusalem, coming down from heaven. And he heard a voice saying:

Look! God's dwelling place is now among the people. . . . They will be His people, and God himself will be with them and be their God. 'He will wipe every tear from their eyes. There will be no more death' or mourning or crying or pain, for the old order of things has passed away. (Revelation 21:3–4)

Jesus, seated like a King on His throne, said, "I am making everything new!"

Hope and joy exploded in John's heart. This news, this picture, this hope was so good that all John could say at the very end of the Bible was, "Amen. Come, Lord Jesus!"

This is *our* future. This is the future of God's creation. Jesus is going to put an end to pain, suffering, tears, and death. One day we will finally be home, with God and with one another, forever! So don't give up. Don't give in. God is going to make everything new.

LET'S DISCUSS TOGETHER

- *What is one reason you are looking forward to heaven?*
- *What is the difference between wishful thinking and hope?*
- *How should Jesus' coming motivate us to live?*

LET'S PRAY TOGETHER

Heavenly Father, we praise You for the hope we have in You. Help us to live for You each day, knowing that someday You are going to return and make everything new. In Jesus' name, amen.

● ● ● ● ● ● ●

For Further Study: Revelation 21–22

ABOUT THE AUTHORS

• • • • • • • • •

P atrick and Ruth Schwenk are the coauthors of *For Better or For Kids: A Vow to Love Your Spouse with Kids in the House* and the creators of TheBetterLifeMinistry.org, which is home to TheBetterMom.com, ForTheFamily.org, and RootlikeFaith.com. Patrick and Ruth have been married for more than twenty years, have four children, and have been in full-time ministry for more than fifteen years. They live in Ann Arbor, Michigan.